CROMWELL'S GARRISON TOWN

Illustration: Christian Tilt

NEWPORT PAGNELL

CROMWELL'S GARRISON TOWN

by
Jack Reynolds

MercuryBooks
Word Go

The Newport Muster is a voluntary, community
organisation in Newport Pagnell whose objectives include
broadening education and local history knowledge

First published in 2013 in the United Kingdom by
Mercury Books, PO Box 3620, MK16 0XQ, England
on behalf of Word Go Limited

web: www.wordgo.org
email: inquiries@wordgo.org

ISBN: 978 0 9541432 5 1

All information is believed correct at the time of writing.

Artwork: Pete Stoneman

Printing: Witley Press Ltd

Front cover helmet illustration: Christian Tilt

Inside covers: 1644 plan of the garrison
– courtesy of the Bodleian Library, Oxford

Acknowledgements

Of the very many people who have helped in this project
and the gathering of material for this book, the author
would especially like to thank the following:

Cheryl Butler

Pete Stoneman

Christian Tilt, Owen Chapman and Katie Barrington

Janet Lane, Gareth Jones and Jac Collins

David Green and Steve Larner

Mark Lancaster MP, Ian Carman and Nick Crank

Colleagues on the Newport Muster group

and most particularly

The Heritage Lottery Fund

Contents

Photographs and images

Thanks for the use of photographs and images are due especially to the Centre for Buckinghamshire Studies, Bedford Borough Council, Cowper & Newton Museum, Newport Pagnell Historical Society, Bucks County Council, the United Reformed Church Newport Pagnell, Bucks Archaeological Society, Cromwell Museum Huntingdon, Bodleian Library Oxford, and the Grafton Regis Millennium Project.

Whilst every effort has been made to identify the ownership or copyright of illustrations reproduced in this publication, in some cases materials have been used which are either freely available in the public domain or appear to be out of copyright (the originator's lifetime +75 years) or where reproduction is allowed under a Creative Commons licence.

In the event of any questions arising as to the ownership or copyright of any materials, photographs or illustrations, please contact Mercury Books, PO Box 3620, MK16 0XQ, England.

Introduction

The 'Hidden Histories' initiative of the Heritage Lottery Fund encourages communities to unearth little-known stories from their past that will be of value to present and future generations.

When a proposition was made to the HLF to support research work on the role of Newport Pagnell as a Front Line garrison in the English Civil War, I felt we had already uncovered enough material to put this forward as a genuine contender. The HLF agreed and now, after a further two years of research assisted by a band of most capable helpers, I am absolutely convinced that the full story deserves to be told.

Mostly poorly recorded or forgotten, the town's five year experience as a fortress in the conflict seems to me to be worthy of regional or national recognition.

Historians agree that the English Civil War, which led to the establishment of the principles of free speech, the ultimate right of Parliament to govern and of equality for all under the law, was one of the most significant episodes in our history. And the garrison at Newport Pagnell certainly played its part.

Oliver Cromwell had a special affinity for the town, fighting alongside its troops, sending his son (the 'joy of his life') to serve there, and summoning most of his New Model Army to meet there on the eve of the Civil War's decisive battle.

▲ **Redcoats in a re-enactment of the historic Naseby battle**

It was a town of traditional attraction to Royalists and Parliamentarians alike, for while Kings and Queens had for centuries come to stay nearby at the royal estate of Grafton, the Roundheads considered it 'fertile ground' for their religious ideologies because of its long association with Puritan and Protestant radicalism.

Both sides saw the garrison as a gateway controlling several of England's most important highways and there was no shortage of interest from senior commanders like the flamboyant Prince Rupert who captured the town for the King, and Lord 'Black Tom' Fairfax and the gritty Londoner Philip Skippon, who won it back for Parliament.

There were also many local characters of note, including neighbourhood rivals Samuel Luke, a diminutive hunchback with a cut-down sword, and the blond adventurer Lewis Dyve, who fought each other for the right to govern the town, and John Bunyan, the most-read religious author who gained much material for his allegorical tales from the town's pubs and brothels.

So why is this story of such evident importance so poorly recorded?

After further research and exploration, my answer is a combination of several things. The fact of the fort's earthworks being washed away over many years is the most obvious; another is because its location, virtually on three county borders made record-keeping problematic, and thirdly because the English Civil War was such a painful and distressing time for many families, they may have wanted to forget rather than to remember it.

The objective of this book is to put the record straight and reveal the whole episode without concealing the less attractive parts.

Cromwell himself had a saying for just such a situation. "Paint it warts and all," he is said to have told the artist Peter Lely who was about to start his portrait.

I have tried to do the same.

– Jack Reynolds, Newport Pagnell
January 2013

Sketch file: Oliver Cromwell (1599–1658)

Along with Winston Churchill, Nelson, Francis Drake and Wellington, Oliver Cromwell consistently wins the vote in polls for the 'greatest-ever Englishman'.

Born in rural Huntingdon to a middle-class farming family, he rose to become the only Commoner in UK history to serve as Head of State.

Spurred on by contempt for King Charles I who was taxing his people unmercifully and frittering away the proceeds, Cromwell believed fervently that the people rather than the monarch held the right to govern and that no one was above the law, principles that are embedded in our society and culture today.

After a year at the Protestant-leaning Sidney Sussex College, Cambridge, and a spell as a backbench MP, Cromwell threw in his lot with a growing band of political dissidents who were prepared to take up arms against the King and the British establishment and culminating in the English Civil War that began in 1642.

Proving himself a brilliant cavalryman and a natural leader, Cromwell climbed the army ranks in less than three years from Captain to Second in Command

▲ **Oliver Cromwell**
Courtesy of the Cromwell Museum, Huntingdon

of Parliament's re-invigorated New Model Army which he mustered at Newport Pagnell in 1645 before comprehensively defeating King Charles I's forces in the decisive Battle of Naseby.

Cromwell recognised Newport Pagnell's vital role for the Parliamentarian cause and kept a close affinity for the town throughout the conflict.

A highly religious believer in hard-line Protestantism, he pledged himself to a 'hearts and minds' campaign to win the people over. He was particularly intolerant of Catholics and led a brutal four-year campaign against them in Ireland for which many will never forgive him.

After the King's execution for treason in 1649, Cromwell led the nation for another decade with considerable popularity as Lord Protector of the Commonwealth or Republic. More than once he was also offered the Kingship but turned it down saying: "I could not seek that which Providence has destroyed."

Although often thought to be a typically dour and serious Puritan, it is said that 'Old Noll' or 'Old Ironsides' as he was nicknamed, was an ebullient character with a good sense of humour. Like many of his contemporaries he smoked a pipe and enjoyed a few glasses of wine, as did his good friend and Governor at Newport Pagnell, Sir Samuel Luke. Another friend there was Rev John Gibbs, the parish priest, who had also studied at Sidney Sussex.

Cromwell had nine children by his wife Elizabeth Bourchier. His first-born son Robert died in 1639 aged only 18. He sent his second, Oliver junior, to serve at the Newport garrison 'to keep an eye on things' but he lost him to camp fever in 1644 aged 21.

After Oliver Cromwell's own death in September 1658 – at home and probably from exhaustion – another son, Richard, succeeded him as Lord Protector but abdicated after a year and went to France in exile.

Note: In this book, today's money value equivalent compared with Civil War times is based on a multiplier of 145. (Source: Research project by Dr Lawrence H Officer, Professor of Economics at University of Illinois, Chicago)

Other sketch files

Timeline

This book is mostly concerned with the Civil War years from 1642 when hostilities broke out between forces loyal to the Crown and those of Parliament at the Battle of Edgehill, to 1649 when King Charles I was executed for treason in a trial ordered by Parliament.

It concentrates especially on the years 1642 to 1646 when Newport Pagnell operated as a military garrison and its soldiers took part in local fighting, battles and events, and until 1648 when the town's fortifications were finally pulled down.

After the King's execution there was the Irish Campaign and the so-called Commonwealth or Republican period which lasted until 1660 when the Crown was restored under Charles II.

1642

August 22	King raises standard at Nottingham, political start of Civil War
October 23	Battle of Edgehill in South Warwickshire, first major clash
October	Aylesbury reverts to Parliament
Oct/Nov	Charles I captures Banbury and sets up his HQ at Oxford
November	Battle of Brentford

1643

April	The Siege of Reading
April	Samuel Luke plunders home of local rival Lewis Dyve
September	1st Battle of Newbury
Various	Northampton and Bedford declare for Parliament
October wk 1	Royalists occupy Newport Pagnell and begin to fortify it. Royalists set up garrison at Towcester
October wk 3	Parliament re-takes Newport Pagnell. Royalists begin to fortify Brill, Grafton & Hillesden estates
November 4	Battle of Olney Bridge
December	Siege of Grafton Manor. Houses of Parliament approve Newport Pagnell fort's finances

1644

January 18	Royalists withdraw from Towcester
January 25	Samuel Luke appointed military governor at Newport Pagnell with Cornelius van den Boom as chief engineer
March	Sacking of Hillesden House
March wk 2	Oliver Cromwell junior dies at Newport Pagnell aged 21
July	Battle of Marston Moor
October	John Bunyan among new recruits at Newport Pagnell
October	2nd Battle of Newbury

1645

June 14	New Model Army gathers at Sherington before Battle of Naseby
June 26	Sir Samuel Luke steps down as Governor of Newport Pagnell
End of Summer	Contingent at Newport Pagnell reduced to 800 foot and 120 horse. Capt Charles D'Oyley is new Newport military Governor

1646	Jan/Feb	Martial law declared at Newport Pagnell as unpaid troops go on rampage
	May/June	Oxford finally falls and Charles I surrenders himself to the Scots (end of phase I of the war)
	August 6	Soldiers stood down at Newport Pagnell and walls to be 'sleighted'
		Call for volunteers for Ireland campaign; Newport Pagnell's guns, ammunition and powder ordered to go there
1647	July	Newport Pagnell's volunteers for Ireland (including Bunyan) are not required and are dispersed
1648	Uncertain	Rev John Gibbs is new parish priest at Newport Pagnell
	May	Fortifications at Newport Pagnell finally demolished; artillery not removed for another year
	August	Battle of Preston
1649	January	King Charles I executed, monarchy abolished and Commonwealth with republican Government begins
	May	*Leveller* leader is chased through Newport Pagnell and shot dead
	August	Cromwell begins four year campaign in Ireland
1651	September 3	Battle of Worcester (end of phase II of the war)
1658	September	Cromwell dies at home in Whitehall and son Richard succeeds him
1659	May	Richard Cromwell abdicates
	August 23	Turncoat George Booth captured at Newport Pagnell
1660	Summer	Monarchy restored. Charles II crowned King (April 1661)
		Cromwell exhumed and posthumously beheaded
		Rev John Gibbs is ousted at Newport Pagnell and establishes today's URC

Other information

- Historians generally agree that the Civil War extended over three periods: 1642–46 when the fighting was mostly in England; 1648–51 across Scotland, Wales and northern England; and 1649–53 in Ireland

- The Royalists did best in the early phases but the Parliamentary forces became increasingly successful, especially after re-training as the New Model Army in 1645

- Oliver Cromwell died in 1658, his son Richard took over but soon stepped down

- The Monarchy was restored under Charles II in 1660

- Figures for war-related deaths and disease are notoriously inaccurate but best estimates are 190,000 in England; 60,000 Scotland and 208,000 in Ireland

Chapter 1: A key location

TO JUDGE the full significance of Newport Pagnell in the English Civil War many historians advocate going back to the Norman Invasion of William the Conqueror in 1066.

When those occupying Frenchmen insisted on knowing all the most notable places of their newly won kingdom, *Neuport* (probably meaning a 'new market') was one of only three towns in the fabled Doomsday Book of 1087 that were recognised as significant centres of trade in Buckinghamshire.

People were drawn to it because the River Ouse (then as now one of the longest rivers in England) was fordable there and because, with its tributary the Ouzel (aka the Lovat), the confluent waters had created a fertile valley rich with crops and pastures and shady woodlands filled with birds and game.

Fulk Paganell, presumably one of William's conquering knights, gave his name to the town and founded a priory nearby called *Tykeford* which he gifted to the abbey of Marmonstier at Tours across the Channel.

Later, when his grandchildren became involved with the place, his grandson Gervase took responsibility for it along with a clutch of other lands in the Midlands, and his granddaughter persuaded her husband's family the deSomerys to build a castle at the northern end to give the inhabitants

▲ **Detail of the Gervase Paganell seal**
From the *Monasticon Anglicanum*

protection on a vantage point high on a knoll of Oxford Clay which overlooked the valley.

What also made the town attractive was the proximity of several Roman roads.

Little more than cart tracks or narrow bridleways in those medieval days, they were nevertheless the only semi-paved, all-weather roads and they were then, as now, some of the most important in the country. Watling Street, the Fosse Way and Ermine Street were routes leading from London northwards to the distant principalities of Wales and Scotland and all brought substantial trade and travellers conveniently close to the town of Newport Pagnell.

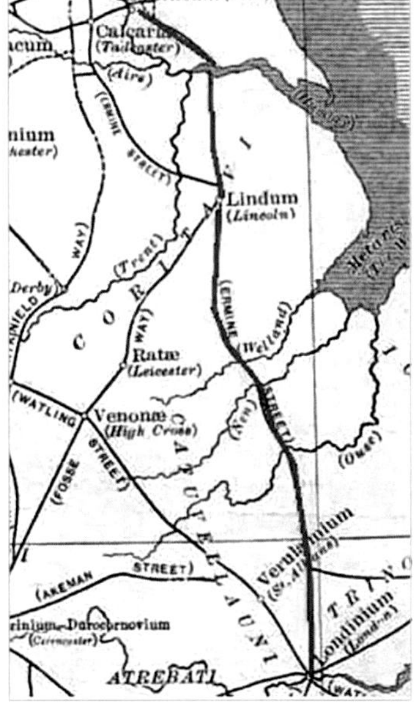

Detail from an old map (not to scale) shows major Roman roads like Watling Street, Fosse Way and Ermine Street all passing close by.

There was also traffic of a quite different kind passing through Newport laterally along the Akeman Street and Icknield Way combination which offered a viable route from the south-west through Oxford and across Middle England's green acres to Cambridge and East Anglia.

This Akerman/Icknield route is mostly overgrown and forgotten today, but it was then an historic 'pilgrims way' favoured by clergy, academics and theologians travelling between the two university cities – and it was undoubtedly due to some of those who followed this trail that Newport would gain its reputation for independent worship and radicalism which led to its receptiveness for being turned into a stronghold of the Parliament's Puritan/Protestant army.

Because of its deteriorated condition, doubts exist over sections of Akeman Street. However, it generally seems to have linked Gloucester with Burford and Faringdon and Aylesbury with a spur via Newport Pagnell that connected with the Icknield Way – one of the most ancient of all tracks in the UK – allowing pilgrims to travel to or from East and West, Oxford and Cambridge.

Those Reformers included the 14th century, russet-gowned and bare-footed lollards (travelling preachers) of Bishop John Wycliffe, master of Balliol, Oxford; John

Harley and Lawrence Humphrey, both apparently born in Newport, who championed the Protestant cause during the 16th century; large numbers of Huguenot and Flemish religious refugees who followed in their tread; and latterly by Rev John Gibbs, the town's Puritan priest during most of the Cromwellian years.

Not surprisingly, as the centuries passed, *Neuport Paganell*'s prominence continued to grow.

Well served by the various thoroughfares for travel and trade, the town enjoyed a rising prosperity and reputation. It was one of only a few towns allowed to mint its own money, it became a centre for courts, law and justice, the site of at least two hospitals and a commercial focus with goods and livestock markets.

The population was small by today's standards, probably fewer than 1,500 in the town itself when the main part of this story begins, and a few more in hamlets in the neighbourhood including Sherington, Olney and Stoke Goldington.

Tykeford with its ancient priory was a separate settlement, as was Marsh End (now Caldecote Street/Willen Road), and Kickles (today's Kickles Farm beyond Bury Field) where there had been evidence of population since Roman times.

Another outlying village which would come to have a profound effect on the town and its future was Grafton, just six miles or so to the north-west of *Paganell* and a pleasant couple of hours by horse across the valley of the meandering Ouse and the shadowy paths of Salcey Forest.

Few people outside of the immediate area in the 15th century would have heard of Grafton, but when the secret came out that Edward IV had wooed and married the commoner Elizabeth Woodfield there, it began a remarkable sequence of royal association with the village and vicinity that lasted for two centuries and would surely rank it alongside the royal estates of Balmoral or Sandringham today.

After the detail of their romance and marriage was eventually made public, Edward continued to visit the Grafton estate, which is wedged in the triangle between Hanslope, Stoke Bruerne and Hartwell and straddles the border of Buckinghamshire with Northamptonshire.

Essentially it was to see his wife and her family – but he also enjoyed hunting through the local woodland.

In those days, when hunting was judiciously enjoyed by the nobility as a bloodsport, there was uninterrupted excitement to be had for miles through the Whittlewood and Whaddon forests to the west around Bicester, Buckingham and Towcester, in the ancient Salcey Forest around Grafton and among the oaks and elms of Rockingham to the north.

Known under the general name of Bernwood, these areas of forest and woodland were conjoined in a region of exceptional hunting country which stretched from Oxford to Stamford. Rather like a forerunner to our Areas of Natural Beauty, Bernwood was designated a Royal Hunting Forest with keepers and wardens to look after it and the deer, boar, and wildfowl that lived within its boundaries.

When his turn came, Edward's grandson Henry VIII continued both the hunting tradition and a love of Grafton. Indeed, he was even more passionate about it than his ancestor.

▲ Roman roads were the only paved, all-weather routes

Henry bought the manor from the Woodville family in 1526 and was soon negotiating with his neighbours to enlarge the estate by 1,000 acres. And that was just the beginning. Next, he called in workmen to extend the house into a virtual palace which doubled up on the one hand as a hunting lodge and on the other as a mansion equally suitable for accommodating meetings of his Privy Council and receptions for visiting foreign ambassadors.

No doubt life with sport and fresh country air must have been a great antidote to the stuffiness of Court, and it wasn't long before the King was taking an annual pilgrimage to Grafton, arriving every year towards the end of August and staying until early October.

At all events, as a mark of his great affection for the location, he commanded that 'Regis' (royal) be added to the village name, an appendage it possesses to this day.

And there was another reason why he liked to be at the Grafton estate. At first in secret, but later very openly, he was able to court Anne Boleyn, the mayor's daughter from Aylesbury, for whom he made the momentous decision to divorce his first wife Katherine of Aragon and break with the Church of Rome.

That historic choice, made in consultation with Cardinal Thomas Wolsey at Grafton in 1529, was to have consequences that still reverberate today and certainly had a bearing on some of the extraordinary events which would follow in the local area, and indeed across the realm, in the Civil War.

With his enormous entourage (he once it is said, travelled with some 5,000 horses, 1,000 soldiers, most members of his Court and 200 tents and pavilions on a 'progress' from London to Grafton via Hatfield and Ampthill in 1540) Henry's arrival in the area year after year would have brought a huge boost to trade in all the local towns of Towcester, *Paganell* and Northampton.

There does not appear to be any record of the king himself being seen in *Paganell* but we do have an account of his daughter, Queen Elizabeth I, passing through the town on one of her own 'progressions' towards the end of the 16th century and it is also reported that she had been granted possession of Newport Manor and the mill at Little Linford in 1551.[1]

The fiery Queen, famous for her red hair and quick temper, did not share her father's great passion for hunting or long visits to Grafton, but she did stay there on three occasions during her reign – in 1564, 1568 and 1575 – and she did share his love for leading her Court, servants and baggage train around the country on frequent hospitality trips to the great houses and families of the day.

Accounts tell of the extraordinary procession snaking slowly through the countryside, stretching for more than a mile and often with more than 1,000 courtiers and followers in her wake.

In some cases, it was said, loyal hosts were bankrupted by the cost of entertaining Queen Bess and her Court when she insisted on extending her stay.

Nevertheless, on this occasion in 1575, it seems probable that something of a smaller party accompanied Elizabeth on her short trip in the horseback procession from Grafton, crossing the Tove at the Castlethorpe Bridge, and then passing the great Manor of *Gothurst* (Gayhurst) just a couple of miles from Newport on the Northampton road.

Gayhurst's foremost mansion, then owned by the Nevills, but soon passing into the hands of the Catholic Digby family, was visible to her on the eastern side although, as it happened, she did not plan to stop there that day.

Elizabeth could not then have had the slightest indication of it of course, but within another generation, Gayhurst and its handsome owner Sir Everard Digby would become the cause of a national sensation when he confessed to organising

---

1   *History and antiquities of the Newport Hundreds*, Ratcliff. p223.

secret meetings of the Gunpowder Plotters there in the unsuccessful plan to blow up Parliament.

Neither could she have forseen that Sir Everard's son John would fight gallantly, but ultimately unsuccessfully, to fend off a greatly superior force of Parliament's men at Grafton Manor after a relentless three-day bombardment in the coming Civil War.

The flame-haired Queen, riding at the head of her entourage, would have looked magnificent in all her finery as the column swept on through Newport's cobbled streets as the people crowded into doorways and hung from windows to watch the pageant pass by.

Perhaps, if it was a Saturday, a colourful market was being held in the main street just as it had been every week for centuries. And perhaps, as she had probably heard from her ladies-in-waiting lately, there would have been much fine lace wear on show, painstakingly created by new Dutch and Flemish settlers from the so-called Low Countries of Europe who had brought new crafts and cultures to the town, new kinds of vegetables and some challenging new Protestant ideologies.

Again, it would not be many years hence when some of those Dutch immigrants showed skills of a different kind – like

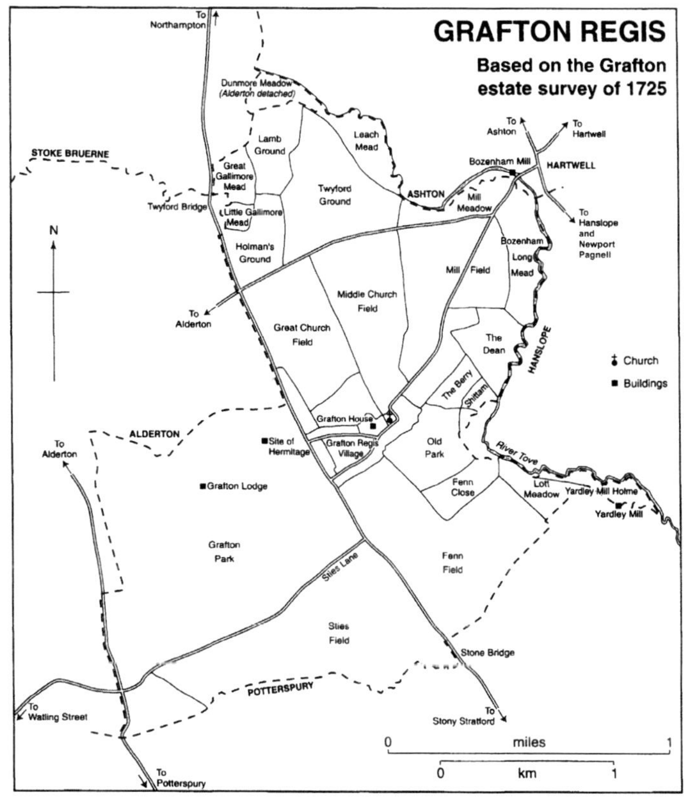

▲ 'Royal' Grafton Regis was just 6 miles from Newport Pagnell

1725 survey by Joseph Collier and William Baker, courtesy of Northants Records Office

how to build earthworks and flood protection systems similar to those in Holland, to turn Newport into a viable fortress.

But how would Queen Elizabeth have known that?

That day, after riding out of town on the eastern side she headed her procession towards North Crawley, about three miles away, where her party was eagerly awaited at the Grange, another local mansion of considerable splendour and which was built for Cardinal Wolsey so he could be near his King at Grafton.

So far, three monarchs, Edward, Henry and Elizabeth, had come to know and enjoy the benefits of this unheralded corner of North Buckinghamshire with its royal estate across the adjacent county border.

And there were two more still to come.

Initially it would be James (James I of England and VI of Scotland), Elizabeth's godson.

James was nearly 40 before Elizabeth's death took him to the throne of England in 1603 and there is much good evidence to show that he, like his predecessors, also knew the Newport area extremely well.

Within a couple of years he presumably felt deep shock when learning that Everard Digby and the Gunpowder Plotters had been meeting at Gayhurst, just outside the Grafton Regis estate, while making plans to blow up both Parliament and him while he was opening the new session in 1605.

But there are credible records to show that he visited the Grafton estate regularly thereafter (typically every two years) from 1608 to 1616 inclusive, often staying at the house with the Duke of Lennox his cousin, or George Villiers subsequently the Duke of Buckingham, and no doubt enjoying their company and friendship while being far from the public gaze.

And there was another reason why the King could make useful advantage of Grafton's obscurity. He would be close to the Buckinghamshire home of Henry Atkins, the royal family's favourite physician.

James had suffered from poor health for most of his life so it would have been singularly fortunate that Dr Atkins should be on hand to treat him locally when the King continued to be dogged by various illnesses and bouts of depression brought on by the nation's growing crisis of debt and his increasingly hostile conflicts with Parliament.

Records of those 'house calls' are naturally confidential, but it is very likely that Dr Atkins, President of the College of Physicians in most years from 1606 to 1625, would have been called on to treat the King at Grafton many times during his periods of convalescence and it is understood that the former Priory building at *Tykeford* plus its adjacent deer park[2] all of which had continued to be held by the Crown estate since Henry VIII's day – were gifted to him in exchange for his unpaid accounts.

In addition, less than a mile from the priory, there is an engraved beam *extant* on a property in St Johns Street which records the visit in 1615 of James's consort, the Queen Anne of Denmark, as a founder of one of the town's charitable hospitals with which Dr Atkins was associated.

It seems clear that Dr Atkins was not only one of the nation's foremost authorities on medical matters, but he had also become a trusted friend of the Royal household. He is said to have 'died rich' in 1635, owning many properties in Newport[3] as well as the Park at *Tykeford*.

10   PELL RECORDS,

sum of 52*l.* for one chain of gold of that value, given by his Highness to the servant of Monsieur de Rohan. By writ, dated 27th of December, 1603 . . . . £52 0 0

Doctor Atkins.} 21*st of April.*—By order, 19th of April, 1604. To Doctor HENRY ATKINS, physician, appointed to make his repair into Scotland, and there to attend the Duke Charles, his Highness's second son, as well for his health while he is there, as for his safe passage up hither to his Majesty's presence, the sum of 100*l.*, for provision of drugs and other things necessary for his said attendance. By writ, dated 14th April, 1604 . . . . 100 0 0

The Earl of Pembroke.} By order, 16th April, 1604. — To the Right Honourable the EARL OF PEMBROKE, the sum of 156*l.* 13*s.* 4*d.*, for one chain of gold given by his Highness unto a servant of the Duke of Guise. By writ, dated 27th of December, 1603 . 156 13 4

▲ Record of £100 being paid to Dr Atkins from James I's 'royal purse' for treatment to him and his son

---

2   For more detail on the Tickford Deer Park see Bucks Gardens Trust (ref 5826)

3   Pastures at Newport called Bury Close, South Edge, Oxmead, Honey Lane and Bury Mead; the Manor and Lordship of Tickford, the Rectory of Newport Pagnell as well as the mansion or priory of Tickford – *Ratcliff ibid p225*

Meanwhile, the money problems that so bedevilled James would now help to bring about the downfall of his son Charles. Dark clouds began to gather almost as soon as Charles had inherited the throne.

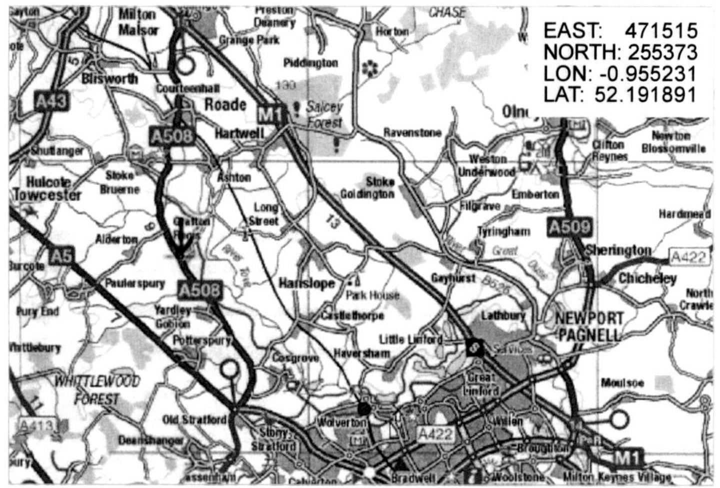

▲ **Contemporary map of the Newport area** – © Ordnance Survey

The Royal Purse was empty, sacrifices had to be made and as the new King became increasingly desperate he was forced to sell off national assets and personal treasures alike, among them the royal estate at Grafton – bought almost exactly 100 years before by his ancestor Henry VIII and now to be mortgaged for not very much to a family called Crane.[4]

Charles I, defying the people and sticking fast to his belief in the inalienable right of kings, was now a long way down the path that would lead to a momentous confrontation with Parliament, a war against his own subjects and eventually to his own summary execution.

How extraordinary then, that so many of the names and places which had taken such prominence in his family's local history... Protestant pilgrims, the green fields of Middle England, *Neuport Paganell*, the Digby family, Grafton Regis, Tickford, Dr Atkins and Dutch engineers would now become so central to it all.

The beginning of the end for the King after whatever history would decide to call it – a Civil War, class struggle, religious conflict, or perhaps a combination of all three – began at Edgehill in 1642.

---

4   Grafton was bought by the royalist Sir Francis Crane in 1628.
    Also see *The Siege of Grafton House* in Chapter 5

Chapter 2: Let battle commence

The green pastures of south Warwickshire one Sunday in October 1642 became the unlikely setting for the first pitched battle of the English Civil War.

Before that fateful day, as an all-out engagement became increasingly inevitable, both sides had spent a year rallying their supporters, recruiting regional organisers and raising their respective armies. Numbers were roughly matched at about 15,000 men,  many of them raw and inexperienced recruits and while the Parliamentarians had more infantrymen and musketeers, the King's forces had more cavalry and artillery.

Before the first shots were fired at Edgehill amid the pleasant rolling countryside between Stratford upon Avon and Banbury, a number of factors had been established.

King Charles I had been forced to quit London (and after Edgehill would set up his army headquarters in Oxford) and he had recruited

◀ **Charles I: forced to quit London**
from a portrait by Antoon van Dyck

Numbers for Parliament would later rise from this early estimate while the Monarchists' would steadily diminish

the services of his dashing German nephew Prince Rupert to lead his cavalry.

For Parliament Robert Devereux, the Earl of Essex, a wise and experienced career soldier now approaching 50, had recruited a so-called 'army of the people' which drew its strength mainly from London and East Anglia.

Even now, right at the outset, it was evident that the English south and east Midlands – bounded as they were in the 'diamond' between Oxford, London, Birmingham and East Anglia – would become the 'theatre' of this most damaging and dispiriting of all wars, the kind described with total irony as a *civil* war where friend turned into enemy and brother became foe, literally from one day to the next.

And the town and hinterland of Newport Pagnell being almost exactly equidistant between the two university cities and between London and Birmingham was placed at its virtual epicentre.

On this historic day at Edgehill there were many from the Newport area who had taken up arms for one side or the other and several among them who would have a lasting influence on events destined to unfold in the months and years to come.

Among them bitter local rivals Sir Lewis Dyve, a flaxen-haired adventurer from Bromham who had

▲ **Centre of the war 'theatre'.**   Graphic: Pete Stoneman. Not to scale

pledged his energies to the King's cause, and his near neighbour, the diminutive Presbyterian Sir Samuel Luke who had thrown in his lot with the Parliamentarians. Unknown to each other among the thousands on the field at Edgehill they would soon be clashing again with deadly intent as their personal feud erupted closer to home.

Here also the dashing Sir John Digby from Gayhurst, son of the disgraced Gunpowder plotter Everard Digby and now

Sketch file: Sir Lewis Dyve (1599–1669)

More of a brawler and fighter than his great local rival Samuel Luke, the bitter neighbours first locked horns when Dyve's home at Bromham, just a few miles up the Bedford road from Newport Pagnell, was plundered by Luke and a troop of anti-Royalists in the Spring of 1643 before the Newport garrison had been established.

The story of Dyve's escape by diving into the Ouse may be apochryphal but he is said to have repeated the trick some years later by leaping into the Thames while being held prisoner in the Tower. At Newport, where the Dyves were connected by marriage to the family of Gunpowder Plotter Sir Everard Digby, he soon gained revenge by seizing Luke's house with help from Digby's son John and 400 cavalrymen.

▲ **Sir Lewis Dyve – Luke's local rival**
After the engraving by Philip Audient
(pub Beds HRS vol XXVII)

Dyve was a personal friend of the King's commander Prince Rupert but after being given the task of capturing Newport Pagnell he made a catastrophic blunder by leaving the place virtually undefended two weeks later and thus allowed Parliament's forces to regain control, a position they never relinquished. A former Oxford university student and much travelled, Dyve was a golden-haired adventurer who was apparently fearless in battle but not so good on administration. Prince Rupert wanted him to command fortresses at Bedford, Northampton and Newport Pagnell, but as with Newport, he swiftly lost power at Bedford and never had control of Northampton at all.

After his local failures, Dyve was sent to fight with Royalist forces in the West Country but he was captured in 1645 and held prisoner for two years. Later, he became a mercenary soldier in exile in France, was often ill and penniless and on his return to the UK found that much of his family's property had been sequestrated and sold. He retired to a small estate in Somerset and is buried there.

Sketch file: Sir Samuel Luke (1603–1670)

▲ **Sir Samuel Luke – Newport's military governor** – © Bedford Borough Council, Moot Hall, Elstow

Local politician, soldier and military commander, Sir Samuel Luke was in charge of the Newport garrison for 18 months until the summer of 1645 during its most active period in the Civil War. A strict disciplinarian with extensive knowledge of the area, he was in many ways an ideal choice to run this crucial centre of the Parliamentarians' campaign.

The oldest son of Sir Oliver Luke, MP, he was brought up at Cople, the family's seat, on Bedford's eastern fringe. He had a personal feud with Sir Lewis Dyve, the local Royalist leader,

which began when he attempted to arrest him (Dyve escaped and Luke was wounded).

In physical stature, Luke was an odd-looking man. Very small ('not much more than dwarf-like,' according to one description) and with a hunch-back,[5] he was nevertheless fiercely determined, energetic and a brave opponent in battle who fought with a specially-shortened sword.

A figure who aroused strong opinions. Birkenhead described him as 'horrible Sir Samuel', while Needham called him a 'scarecrow' but added: 'as a commander he was short in size but tall in courage and resolution.'

A devout Presbyterian and profoundly anti-Catholic,

---

5 'He looks like a snail with a house upon his back,' said an anonymous writer in the contemporary newsletter *Mercurius Menippeus. The Censor* No XV July 1823 p28. Also, he was 'deformed and dwarfish' – *A History of Newport Pagnell* (Staines, 1842)

Sir Samuel insisted on a regime of religious vigour during his time in charge at Newport and, as well as often leading his troops on active skirmishes and operations, he cultivated a network of spies and informants which enabled him to provide invaluable information on Royalist plans and troop movements as Parliament's chief scoutmaster. "The enemy eat, sleep, drink not, whisper not, but (that) he can give us an account of their darkest proceedings," it was reported by *Mercurius Britanicus,* a popular news-sheet.

Luke's appointment ended after Newport had played a significant role in the rendezvous of Parliamentary forces before the pivotal Battle of Naseby but he then began a two year fight of his own to win more than half a million pounds (in today's values) of outstanding pay.

He was apparently the character *Hudibras* in the best-selling satirical work of that name by Samuel Butler, Luke's one-time personal assistant, which left him deeply embittered.

He died in 1670 at Cople and was buried there.

evidently at ease with King Charles' cohorts as he added his prowess with the cavalry horse to his skills as a renowned swordsman. Alongside him, Sir Edmund Verney from Hillesden, who would die heroically on the blood-drenched battlefield defending the King's standard, his arm cut clean off it was said, with the hand still clutching the flagstaff.

Among Parliament's men was 'half an army' or so it seemed who had marched up from their rendezvous at the fortress of Northampton with a regiment of the green-coated infantrymen from Aylesbury. That town was already a self-declared stronghold for Parliament where John Hampden, a cousin of the young Oliver Cromwell ⬤ was fast earning a reputation as one of the nation's greatest exponents of free speech and, consequently, one of the King's severest critics.

In the event, when the mists had cleared above those fields at Edgehill, revealing about the same number (2,000) of dead and wounded on both sides, neither the King and his flamboyant Prince Rupert, nor the Earl of Essex and Sir Thomas (Black Tom) Fairfax, commanders of the Parliamentary forces, were able to claim victory.

But perhaps more importantly for the annals of history, this first battle had proved that proud Englishmen from the south Midlands as elsewhere were prepared to stake their lives on the idea that the monarch had, or did not have, a 'divine right' to rule and whether anyone – even a king – could hold themselves above the law.

At its heart, and despite its historic importance, there were many more consequences of the battle at Edgehill than the outcome itself, one of the most profound being the national attention it focused on the importance of the Midlands region.

In the 'false war' before Edgehill, Northampton ⬤ had been among the first to declare which side they would be on. "The general feeling in the town was strongly in favour of the Parliament when the shadow was beginning to darken the land," an account would later reveal (*Life of Col Whetham* p48).

⬤ Oliver Cromwell apparently arrived too late to take any part in the action at Edgehill. Within another year however he was rapidly reaching hero-status as the commander of a cavalry regiment within the Eastern Association known as the 'Ironsides' and by 1645 he had re-trained and professionalised the Parliamentary troops into the New Model Army.

⬤ The Northampton garrison was also useful to the Parliamentary cause for other reasons. The town's famous leather-workers kept the Roundhead army in boots and shoes throughout the war.

Sketch file: Prince Rupert, Count Palatine of the Rhine (1619–1682)

Prince Rupert the dashing cavalier
from a portrait by Simon Verelst
(Commoner file © free)

A flamboyant soldier and brilliant horseman who spent his early life fighting in Spain and Germany, he was a full nephew of Charles I who answered his uncle's call for help and was appointed Commander of the King's cavalry aged 23.

Something also of a scientist and inventor, he was on the one hand quick-thinking, brave and energetic but alternately hot-headed, impatient and temperamental.

Banished from the UK after Charles' trial and execution, he returned after the Restoration and was appointed an admiral and colonial governor.

Initially placed under the command of Lord Brooke, son of the Earl of Warwick, an order was immediately made to repair the town gates, install drawbridges, and restore walls and ramparts of the former castle fortifications.

So, even before the war ignited at Edgehill, Parliament's first defendable fixed supply base in the region was already secure and another would shortly follow.

At Aylesbury, as accounts later confirmed, a body of Prince Rupert's cavalry, still flush from their efforts at Edgehill, detoured into the town as they made their way back towards Oxford.

Perhaps they simply wanted to teach him a lesson but whatever the reason, the Prince's men determined to take on the town's most famous resident John Hampden, Cromwell's cousin, who had become a thorn in the side of the Royalist cause by his adamant campaigning against the spendthrift King's hated 'Ship Money' tax.

As it happened, Hampden would be dead within six months, killed by a stray musket shot, but on this day at Aylesbury when the word went round that Prince Rupert's men were on their way, Hampden's infantry and pikemen quickly set up such a solid defence on the approach at Holman's Bridge they were soon put to flight.

As a result the important town of Aylesbury, probably the only town in Buckinghamshire with a larger population than Newport's and with a castle, courts and jail, was lost to the King and became a vital bridgehead for the forces of Parliament being closest to the Royal headquarters at Oxford and a forward centre for supplies of men, weapons and ammunition.

In the flurry of propaganda posters that followed Edgehill, King Charles and Rupert boasted they had won the war's first battle but in reality the loss of Aylesbury and the entrenched hostility at Northampton were seen by many as being pivotal. Newport itself was not involved as yet, but the end-stops of a front line across the all-important theatre of war in the Midlands had now been firmly established for the Parliamentarian side and this would be argued as being a major contributory factor in their campaign to come.

Inevitably in an era when more often than not, communications were on a parchment proclamation read out by the town crier and when roadways were frequently no more than cart-tracks and transport was by horse and carriage, events moved frustratingly slowly. It was a challenge for both sides to increase the number of recruits and a massive effort to move large units of men and equipment over any distance.

There were few major confrontations over the next twelve months and even less with a decisive outcome. But the most notable came in November 1642 at Brentford where the Royalists declared themselves winners, at the siege of Reading, then in the following April the forces of Parliament hailed victory and at the first Battle of Newbury in September 1643, although neither side was entitled to claim the spoils, where both armies enjoyed some success.

As the months passed and the situation polarised, came an agonising time for making decisions about which side to support. As so often in civil wars, the answer frequently had dramatic consequences for family, friends and neighbours.

In the Newport Pagnell area the Catholic Throckmorton family from Newton Underwood declared for the King along with Sir John Digby of Gayhurst, his neighbours the Tyringhams, the Dayrells of Lillingstone Dayrell, the Cranes of Grafton Regis, Lady Farmer from Easton Neston and Spencer Lucy of Haversham, the Longvilles of Wolverton, the Chester family of Chicheley (excepting for son Henry) and Dr Napier of Great Linford.

For the Parliamentarians important supporters included the Bennett family of Calverton and Sir William Andrews of Lathbury a notable ally since his substantial property with land and stabling was no more than a short pistol shot from the town.

The Manor at Lathbury would also feature in Newport Pagnell's history nearly three centuries later when Ian Fleming, author of the James Bond books, studied there for his entry into Sandhurst Army College before WWII when it was a 'crammer' educational establishment for sons of the wealthy.

In this period of consolidation in 1642–3 every family in the land was coming to terms with the reality that the nation was at war with itself.

For those who did not declare, some, like the brilliant scientist Sir Kenelm Digby from Gayhurst, another son of the Gunpowder Plotter, fled to safe havens abroad. Others, and there were a great many of them, hoped not to fight for either side but to continue with their lives as best they could, paying the levies and taxes demanded of them, and suffering the consequences as their homes were raided for food and supplies by marauding patrols.

But two local men stood out, with their personal determination to make a mark in the conflict, Sir Lewis Dyve of Bromham and his near-neighbour Sir Samuel Luke.

Sketch file: Sir John Digby (c.1605–1645)

Just a babe in arms at Gayhurst House, Newport Pagnell, when his father Sir Everard Digby, the Gunpowder Plot conspirator, was executed, John grew up to be a fervent supporter of Charles I in the Civil War. Described as an exceptional swordsman and immensely strong, he reached the rank of Major General.

When Newport Pagnell was first taken by the King's forces he was tasked with raising a local cavalry regiment and after they lost it he was charged with defending the royal estate at Grafton Regis.

Sir Samuel Luke's Letter of Warrant for the Safety of the Lady Digby.

[IBID.]

THESE are to will and require you upon sight hereof to forbeare to prejudice the Lady Digby, of Gotehurst, in the County of Bucks,ᵃ by offering any attempt or violence to her owne person or the persons of any of her family, plundring her house or Parke, rifling her goods, or by spoyling or taking away any of her horses or cattle, as you will answer the contrary at your perills, without speciall warrant from his Excell. the Governour of this Garrison for the time being, or the Comittees of this County appointed by the Parliament.   Given under my hand the 4th day of June, 1644.

SAM. LUKE.

To all Colonells, Lieut. Collonells, Captaines, Liefts. and all Officers and Souldiers of the Army, and others whom it may concerne.

▲ **Luke provided Lady Digby with a Safe Passage warrant**

Forced to surrender after a three-day siege, he was taken under guard to Lathbury and then to the Tower in London but subsequently released in a prisoner swap. He re-joined the King's army only to receive a gunshot wound at the Battle of Langport in Somerset from which he died a horribly lingering death 31 days later.

Despite the Digby family's loyalty to the King, Sir John's older brother Sir Kenelm Digby (1603–1665) a pronounced Catholic, statesman, scientist and astrologer, fled to France and spent the war in exile. Their mother Lady Mary Digby (nee Mulsho) was allowed to continue living at Gayhurst throughout the war and Sir Samuel Luke, Newport's governor, chivalrously issued her with a 'safe passage' pass.

Both would have a very significant influence on the town of Newport Pagnell.

After flinging themselves into the war at Edgehill, both men were jockeying for more senior positions in their respective armies by the Spring of 1643 and since their families knew each other well, it can be supposed that the feud between them was both personal and acrimonious.

The first to strike was Sir Samuel Luke. The virulently anti-monarchist son of Bedford MP Sir Oliver Luke from Cople on Bedford's eastern fringe, Luke set out in April 1643 with a cohort of troops to arrest Dyve at his home beside the Ouse at Bromham.

It was a swift affair. Luke, a diminutive man in size but large in ambition, was wounded in the swordfight that ensued and Dyve, who had probably received warning of the impending attack, made good his escape by jumping into the river and swimming to safety. 🗨

Six months later, when Newport Pagnell was being turned into a garrison by the King's forces and Dyve had been installed as its first Governor, he sought revenge by taking a party of 400 cavalrymen to Luke's house, hoping to arrest him. In the event, although they plundered his house, Luke escaped. The chance was gone and (see Chapter 3) Luke would later take over the Governorship at Newport and have a big say in enabling the garrison to make a highly significant contribution to the Roundheads' ultimate success.

In summary, by October 1643 at the end of the first year of hostilities, the headcount of the Parliamentary forces had risen to about 25,000 while the King's had stayed at around 15,000 with strongest support in Wales and the West Country.

It meant that the South Midlands had indeed become the battleground over which the military commanders would have to make their best tactical decisions in the months ahead. The balance of power seemed finely poised. Parliament already had garrisons established at Northampton and Aylesbury while the

🗨 Dyve several times escaped captivity by swimming to safety but it is unclear whether his name has any connection with the modern aquatic term. According to several sources the verb to dive derives from the old English word dyfan.

King's powerbase was entrenched at Oxford and the nearby redoubt at Banbury.

The next requirement would be for one side or the other to consolidate full control, but which side would it be? And who would occupy Newport Pagnell, the town at the very centre of this all-important region?

The nation would not have to wait long to find out.

Sketch file: Robert Devereux, Earl of Essex (1591–1646)

▲ **The Earl of Essex sent the order**

from a portrait by Marcus Gheeraerts the Younger

Chief commander of the Parliamentary army from 1642–46, the sternly Protestant Earl was a career soldier who spent his early years fighting in Germany and the Low Countries where he became proficient in continental war tactics.

Appointed by the House of Commons to raise an army in 1642 he led its forces with varying success at Edgehill, Brentford, Reading and Newbury and gave the orders to Sgt Major Philip Skippon to march his London divisions up to Newport Pagnell and recapture the town in October 1643.

Eventually over-shadowed by the achievements of Oliver Cromwell and Sir Thomas Fairfax, culminating in their landmark victory at Naseby in 1645, he resigned his commission in the following year.

Chapter 3: Establishing the Front Line

The bright autumn days of October 1643 brought arguably the most significant turning point in the first, and most vigorous, phase of the Civil War and especially for Newport Pagnell.

The town's strategic importance in the unfolding drama had been growing month by month. Here was the centre of the self-same 'diamond' between the King's forces at Oxford and Parliament's powerbase of East Anglia, and between London and the south, and Birmingham and the major cities beyond, and the strategists on both sides were very much aware of it.

Safe supply lines, the roads or waterways along which armies send reinforcements of men, weapons or provisions to their forward troops, are critical in warfare, and never more than in this domestic confrontation. So Newport Pagnell's location on one of the longest rivers in England and its ability to command several of the nation's major roads made its value outstanding.

In their debates over strategy and tactical planning, advisers argued firmly with Prince Rupert and the King's commanders that swift action should be taken to secure the town, while those who counselled the Earl of Essex and his second-in-command Lord ('Black Tom') Fairfax on the

Parliamentary side, also eyed the prize. But on this occasion, it was the Cavaliers who put a plan into action first.

With increasing frequency the King had come to trust no one more with his most crucial assignments than Prince Rupert, his German nephew whose daring and apparently endless energy were already legendary. And so it was at the beginning of this fateful October that the dashing cavalry commander rode out at the head of 'a mighty force of 2,000 horse and 700 foot' with the specific aim of overrunning each of the principal towns in the Midlands 'war theatre' and setting them up as fortresses for the King.

Unfortunately, as history records, the result was not all that he wished.

The first blow came at Northampton where the Prince evidently under-estimated the defensive strength of the garrison and found his horsemen's charges were roundly repulsed by artillery fire from behind the thick stone walls and withering volleys of musket shot from the high palisades.

Taking the dead and wounded with him, the commander wasted no time in wheeling away towards Bedford where the outcome was more to the Prince's liking. Sentries and soldiers in the poorly-defended castellated area and numbering only about 300 were soon overcome and after a number of civic dignitaries were 'signed up' with gold coin, it was thought that the King would be able to rely on the town's reluctant allegiance, if only for a few days.

And so the Prince's cavalry rode on, no doubt a formidable sight, out across the river bridge towards Newport Pagnell, just a handful of miles through woodland and open fields and past the family estate at Bromham of the ambitious Sir Lewis Dyve who had already fought alongside the Prince on several battlefields and was solidly devoted to the Royal cause.

An occupation of Newport, Sir Lewis observed, would be a handsome prize to take back to their Sovereign and, as at Bedford, the raiding Cavaliers encountered little more than token resistance when their overwhelming numbers took the

Illustration by Christian Tilt

town by surprise and allowed them to assume swift control of its most important buildings and facilities.

So far, so good. It was just as they had hoped and planned. Within another couple of weeks they fully expected to turn the town into a new fortified command centre with a thousand men providing a vital focus for the Crown's forces in the region and, as their newly-published propaganda posters proclaimed, enabling them to cut off the Roundheads' supply routes of 'meat and fat cattle', from the farms of East Anglia, to their supporters in London.

After one more burst, to the ancient Roman town of Towcester (also known as *Toster* or *Toxiter*) where Rupert ordered the old stone walls to be rebuilt and a moat/ditch to be dug around the place, the German cavalryman journeyed back to Oxford with a happy heart and much encouraging news for his uncle, the King.

The mission's successful result, he concluded, was that the towns of Bedford, Newport Pagnell and Towcester were now within the Royal fold and even if Aylesbury and Northampton were still beyond the King's reach at least he had established a control base within that all-important 'diamond' of the south Midlands from which they could expand.

Back at Newport Pagnell the Royalist commanders were wasting no time in consolidating their occupation.

Sir John Digby, the Gayhurst veteran of several battles in the Royal cause and now back among the fields and hedgerows of his youth, was charged with raising a substantial force of cavalry from the surrounding neighbourhood.

Then, such were the hopes for using the town as a strategic centre, Sir Charles Lloyd, General-in-chief of engineers on the Royal side, was swiftly summoned. The General, who had learned fortress-building skills from previous military campaigns abroad, was expected to put them to good use here and would work with Lewis Dyve, the town's self-appointed governor immediately setting out to press-gang hundreds of locals into building the fortifications General Lloyd proposed.

Sir Charles Lloyd (c.1602–1661) the military engineer, was appointed in charge of all fortifications for the Crown. At one time, Parliament tried to hire him for more money. He refused, but his pay rapidly fell behind and he was forced to petition for destitution at the Restoration.

A report stated: 'he compelled the locals to throw up earthworks in Bury Field, to build a stone wall in Marsh End and to draw water round the town to better strengthen and fortify it.'[6]

6   *History of Newport Pagnell* (P68, Staines, 1842)

Sketch file: Philip Skippon (c.1600–1660)

One of the most distinguished soldiers in the Parliamentary army, he was sent by the Earl of Essex to re-capture Newport's garrison in October 1643 and his orange and green-uniformed soldiers of the London Trained Bands marched in virtually unopposed. Within three months, Major Gen Skippon had strengthened the town's defences, repulsed attempts to reclaim the place by Prince Rupert, commander of the King's forces, and taken the initiative with a number of important actions including the successful siege of Grafton House near Towcester.

An uncomplicated Puritan, career soldier, popular and revered by his men, Skippon made certain that Newport's importance had been thoroughly established by the time he handed over to Samuel

▲ **Skippon: career soldier**
Courtesy of the Bucks Arch. Soc.

Luke as Governor early in 1644. He was also responsible for introducing Cornelius van den Boom, the fortifications engineer whose work he had previously seen in Holland. Skippon went on to become a senior training officer when the New Model Army was formed in 1645. He was badly wounded at Naseby and came close to death but recovered and often returned to the Newport area.

In 1655 he was virtually gifted the sequestrated manors of Water Eaton, Whaddon and Winslow for £1,000 (although they were worth 10 times that). He then 'parcelled them up' into small lots and had sold twenty of them by Christmas 1657 for more than £12,000 (£1.75m today) to sitting tenants, local farmers or back to their previous owners.[7]

During the Commonwealth period, he was several times returned as MP for Kings Lynn but did not take to politics and spoke in the House very rarely.

7   *The Sales of Royalist Land during the Interregnum* by Joan Thirsk (*Economic History Review*, New series 1952, vol 5/2)

It was just a matter of time, Prince Rupert no doubt supposed, before the fortress at Newport would become one of the brightest jewels in the Royal campaign. But he was wrong.

Even as the local labour force, many quite unwillingly, were raising their shovels to build new earthwalls and bastions under the Cavaliers' command, one of the craggiest and best-respected soldiers in the Roundhead army was being detailed in London to lead an expeditionary force to Newport tasked with re-taking the town.

The plan agreed by the Earl of Essex and his number two Lord Fairfax was that Major Gen Philip Skippon, one of the most experienced and capable soldiers in the Parliamentary army, would take several divisions of his Green and Orange-coated London Trained Bands, and march them up to Newport along the Watling Street via St Albans and Dunstable.

Accounts are disappointingly scarce of what they found when they reached the town. It was incredible, there were virtually no Cavalier soldiers in the place and Sgt Major Skippon's troops re-gained control of one of the most important towns in the region without a fight.

Why the defence at Newport Pagnell was abandoned after being under Royal control for less than two weeks Ⓠ remains one of the great unexplained riddles of the whole Civil War. Some of the suggested reasons to be found in later accounts and records are as follows.[9–15]

Ⓠ The royalist occupation of Newport actually lasted for 12 days from October 16 1643 to October 28 according to Prof Ian Beckett – *Guide to Bucks County Museum Civil war Exhibition 2004/5*

9   'Dyve misunderstood a badly-worded order to withdraw,' *Battles & Generals in the Civil War 1642–51*, HCB Rogers, p111

10 'Word came that a badly-needed ammunition train had arrived at Buckingham and the force was summoned down there to guard its passage back to Newport…' *anon*

11 'One of the strangest incidents of the war. Sir Frederick Cornwallis at Oxford ordered him to pull out of town with all baggage to reinforce the Royalist presence elsewhere…' *Rupert, Prince Palatine*, Eva Scott (Archibald Constable, 1900)

12   'Dyve unfortunately mistook his orders and … moved away to
     Prince Rupert's base at Stony Stratford' (a field command post).
     The Last Skirmish, Paul Woodfield, Festival 350, p21

13   *Steps of John Bunyan,* Vera Brittain p79 suggests false rumours
     might have been spread in revenge because 'Dyve issued warrants
     requiring the local population to work on the defences and for
     them to provide money and provisions [to his troops]'.

14   *History & Antiquities of the Newport Hundreds,* Oliver Ratcliff
     (Cowper Press 1900) suggests that the Cavaliers 'quitted their
     post because their numbers would have been unequal'.

15   Other sources claimed the town 'was not given up without
     resistance', although there was no further substantiation. Yet
     another theory suggested Skippon and the London men's
     formidable reputation meant the defenders' resolve became
     weaker as the city bands got nearer.

Speculation was rife. It was certainly likely that only a few
Cavalier soldiers had been detailed to defend the town.
The Royalists had planned to man the garrison with about
1,200 troops but that was not expected for some time. At this
point, although Prince Rupert would have left behind some
of his taskforce of cavalry and officers at each of the towns
he commandeered, since they were from his own troop he
would have been loathe to leave very many.

Instead, Sir John Digby had been ordered to recruit local
horse and infantrymen, but again, he would say he had not
had much time to do so.

Neither is it likely that the occupying forces would have
received much co-operation from the townspeople. Newport
had a long history of non-conformity and independence and
it is certain its everyday citizens would have felt a far greater
affinity with the artisans of Northampton and East Anglia
than the intelligencia and hitherto ruling classes of Oxford.

It also seems that Lewis Dyve press-ganged local labour into building duties, and this could have fed resentment.

On the other hand, perhaps that theory about the impending arrival of Sgt Major Skippon's forces causing the Cavaliers to simply take fright and desert was right after all?

Without doubt, it would have been an imposing sight to witness the 'trained bands' of green and orange-uniformed London men, a private militia of hardened 'soldiers of fortune' with a fearsome reputation as they slogged their way up the old Watling Street Roman road, being reinforced on the route by red-jacketed colleagues from Hertfordshire and some green-coated musketeers from Aylesbury. A formidable array of armed and disciplined fighting men whose progress will have most certainly reached the ears of those few guardians at Newport.

It also seems likely that other reports, which stated 'the town was not given up without resistance' may have been straight-forward face-saving propaganda since there were no accounts of casualty numbers, a sure sign in this war of rumours, that there were none.

However it must also be likely that the desertion theory was wide of the mark since both Dyve and Digby the local commanders were tough characters who would go on to prove their courage many times over in this war.

At any event, and whether they could believe their good fortune or not, Major Gen Skippon and his men from London marched into Newport Pagnell to a far quieter reception than they had dared expect.

Soon, as news of the bungle reached Oxford, the reaction was thunderous. Prince Rupert, reporting to his King, was described as being 'incandescent with rage' and resolved to take immediate revenge by returning to Newport in the following week and do 'whatever was necessary' to win it back.

But he was already too late (see Chapter 4). Skippon, using all his experience, brought in local administrator Samuel Luke and top soldiers, Captains Harvey and Wilson and put himself in charge as master of works.

With great speed he set up a ring of outposts around the town, which actually caught Prince Rupert out on his revenge attack the following week, and he successfully lobbied for a reinforcing regiment of men from the Hertfordshire militia to be sent to the garrison in the following month.

By December, just eight weeks after he had marched into the town, Skippon noted with great satisfaction that the Houses of Lords and Commons passed an official Bill of support for Newport Pagnell underlining its high status in the war. It began: 'The Lords and Commons, taking into their serious considerations the great importance of the town of Newport Pagnell...'[16] 🔵

And by January, when he went back to London after handing over control at Newport to Samuel Luke as the garrison's military Governor, his job was done.

🔵 Among the stipulations was that Newport's garrison town should be strongly fortified, manned by 1,200 foot soldiers and 300 horse, costs kept within a budget of £4,000 per month (about £7m pa in today's terms), and the Governor given powers to force 'the richer sort of inhabitants' to buy weapons for the poorer in times of need. The level of detail was remarkable even providing for a civilian town mayor at an allowance of 9 shillings per diem.

16 HoC Dec 18 1643 'Ordinance for the erecting and maintaining of a garrison at Newport Pagnell...' *History & Antiquities of the Newport Pagnell Hundreds*, Oliver Ratcliff p219 (Cowper Press, 1900)
See extract on next page.

" The Lords and Commons, taking into their serious consideration the great importance of the town of Newport Pagnell, in the county of Buckingham. to the safety of the county adjacent, and of all the associated counties under the command of the earl of Essex, do ordain and order, that the said town shall be strongly fortified and furnished with all necessary provisions for a garrison ; and that the counties of Bedford, Hertford, Northampton, Cambridge with the Isle of Ely, Suffolk Norfolk with the county and city of Norwich, Huntingdon, and Essex, and the Three Hundreds of Newport, shall joyne in the charge of the said garrison and fortifications, for the raising of £1,000, viz.,—in the county of Bedford, £187/10/-, Hertford, £125 ; Northampton, £125 ; Huntingdon, £45 ; Cambridge with Ely, £80 ; Suffolk, £125 ; Essex £125 ; Norfolk with the city and county of Norwich, £125 ; and in the Three Hundreds of Newport, £62/10/-; that if the said fortifications shall arise to more than £1,000 the same shall be raised in counties and Hundreds above said, according to the proportion aforesaid ; and in the said counties and Hundreds, the monthly sum of £4,000 ; Bedfordshire, £750 ; Herts, £500 ; Northampton, £500 ; the Three Hundreds of Newport, £250 ; Huntingdon, £180; Suffolk, £500 ; Cambridge and the Isle of Ely, £320 ; Norfolk and city and county of Norwich, £500 ; Essex, £500 ; and that the first month shall be accounted from 1 Dec. 1643, last past ; that the county of Bedford, within fourteen days after passing this ordinance, shall send into it the said garrison 225 able and armed men for souldiers ; Hertford, 150: Northampton, 150 ; the Three Hundreds of Newport, 75 ; Huntingdon, 45 ; Cambridge with Ely, 105 ; Suffolk, 150 ; Essex, 150 ; Norfolk with Norwich, 150, like able men ; all men so sent in being 1,200, to be put into one regiment, under the command of such Governor and Officers as his excellency shall appoint, and shall be from time to time recruited for the keeping of the said regiment full according to the proportion speci- fied. That the committees for the weekly assessments already established by Parliament, or any two or more of the said committees respectively, shall have power to leavie and raise the money for the fortifications and maintenance of the said garrison for provision of arms, ammunition, and other incident charges, with the best equality, they, or any two or more of them respectively, can, upon each several parish, township or place, &c. according to the rule of weekly assessments for the Parliament Army, and shall send forth their warrants to the High Constables, or such other persons as they shall think fit, &c., with power to enforce obedience to their commands, and to enable them to presse such able men as they see good for the said service, according to an ordinance of both Houses of Parliament, &c. That a treasurer shall be chosen by the committee of the several counties, who shall give his personal and constant at- tendance in the said garrison, and for his pains have an allowance of 5/- per diem, and with appointment of Muster Masters, with like allowance. That the Field Officers and Captains shall make up their recruits of arms out of the pay of the officers and soldiers of the companies of the garrison ; and the Governor of Newport to *compel all the inhabitants of that town, able of body, within the line, to list themselves under command,*and do duty in time of seige, alarum, and assault onely ; and the said gov- ernor, and any three of the committee of the said garrison, shall have power to charge the richer sort of inhabitants with so many arms, for arming the poorer sort, as they shall be of ability to provide ; *and if any disobey, he and the committees shall have power to put them and their families out of the garrison ;* also to have power to appoint a Maior of the town of Newport to receive and give orders, and to command the townsmen, in the time of seige, alarum, or assault, and with an allowance of 9/- per diem ; the aforesaid sum of £4,000 a month being allotted for 300 horse, with their officers, during such time as they shall continue for the safe guard of the garrison, and the preservation of the parts and counties adjacent, &c."

Around the Front Line fortresses

Newport Pagnell

Unlike each of its sister fortresses in the south Midlands, Newport Pagnell did not have a castle, even one in disrepair, on which to base its new, defensive requirements. Once, the Someries Castle had kept guard over the town, but the stone from that had long ago been used to re-build the parish church. Instead, Newport had to start virtually from scratch, throwing up a defensive shield of earthwork walls and ramparts. It wasn't cheap and it wasn't very permanent with storms and river floods a constant hazard, but it was quick to do, and worth the effort, both sides concurred, because of its hugely important geographical location.

Lathbury Manor, just outside the town's walls was another benefit. Owned by Parliamentary supporter Sir William Andrews, it was extremely useful as stabling for cavalry horses and as quarters for the men. Another part was converted into a jail for detaining prisoners.

With a full complement of 1,500 men, the garrison effectively doubled the size of the town, placing a huge strain on local resources. Samuel Luke the Parliamentarian Governor, kept order by a strict regime of military administration and religious devotion provided by no fewer than seven preaching 'divines' and church services at least twice daily.

Troops were continuously deployed back and forth on patrols, skirmishes and reinforcement duties and there were times when Luke feared the town was severely under-manned. He also faced threats of mutiny from soldiers, including officers, who were frequently unpaid, under-fed and poorly clothed. Because of its central location, Newport was used as the rendezvous point for much of Cromwell's army prior to the Battle of Naseby in 1645 when many thousands of troops massed in the vicinity.

Samuel Luke was succeeded as Governor by Col Charles D'Oylie, who was not a success, and then by the hard-line zealot Col John Venn.

Northampton

Nathaniel Whetham, a west country Major in the dragoons, was appointed Governor of Northampton in early 1642 and immediately set about repairing and strengthening the town's 300-year-old castle walls which were 'broad enough for six men to walk abreast.'

The town had declared for Parliament right from the outset, a hardly surprising outcome considering its tradition for religious non-conformity.

With five massive main gates and water ditches fed by sluices from the River Nene, Whetham soon had the place in good shape to defend itself. How wise he was! Next year, Prince Rupert and a large force of Royalists attempted to seize the town but they were quickly beaten off by withering fire from inside the walls and several barrages of heavy artillery from the castle mound.

Thereafter Northampton acted as a secure fortress, guarding the supply routes north and south, sending out troops to reinforce Roundhead operations and for important joint assignments with forces at Newport Pagnell such as the seizing of Grafton House and the siege of the Castle at Banbury.

After the main action was over, Whetham bought a 700-acre estate of sequestrated land in his beloved Somerset and ended his military career as Governor of the Portsmouth garrison.[17]

Like Newport, Northampton was similarly predisposed to the Parliamentarian's Puritan creed. It was called the 'Mecca of English non-conformists' and had 'a recurring tradition of defiance of authority' according to *VCH Northampton: vol 3* (1930) pp1–26

---

17 Sources include: *Northampton – A Parliamentary garrison 1642–47 of national importance*, E. Mids Archaeological Research Framework (David Hall) and VCH *Northampton – vol 3* (1930) p1–26

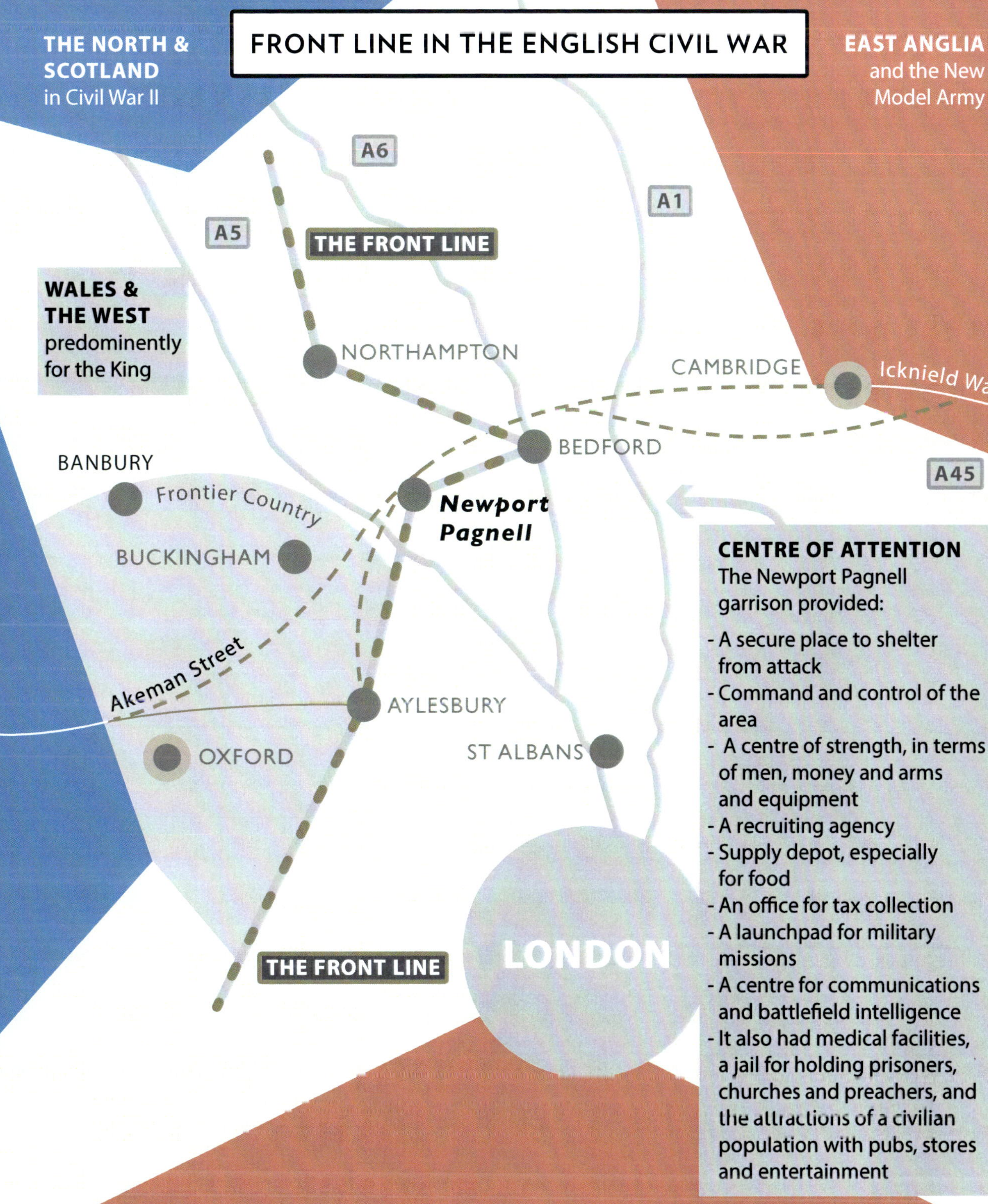

▲ After King Charles abandoned the capital he set up his Court and Army HQ at Oxford while the Parliamentarian forces were strongest in London and East Anglia. The Front Line in the conflict, including the garrison at Newport Pagnell, was in-between. Graphic: Pete Stoneman – a contemporary adaptation, not to scale.

Bedford

At the start of hostilities it seemed that Royalists, led by their local leader Sir Lewis Dyve, would have the town's fortress to themselves. Rebuilding on the remains of the old castle gave the defences a focal point, but again, support for Parliament was under-estimated and at an early moment Roundhead forces led by Col. Montague re-took control by an undisclosed 'cunning stratagem'.

The town was, in those days, about the same size as neighbouring Newport. It commanded another of the main routes north to south and also, crucially, the road from Cambridge and East Anglia which therefore guaranteed safe passage for Cromwell's troops and supplies. Additionally, the fields of the fertile Ouse plain were a major cereal crop producer and there was an extensive trade up and down the river. The town was useful too, for its sizeable jail to house war prisoners and as a major provider of quarters for troops awaiting forward postings.

Although there were local flurries of activity from time to time, the main skirmishes were elsewhere and this produced a ready supply of volunteer fighting men who wanted to see action in other places, like Newport for example. Its defenders were officially disbanded in 1646 but the town's location made it a logical centre of administration for Cromwell and he experimented with it as a regional headquarters for the following year. All military activities there ceased in 1647.

Aylesbury

Once the King had decided to leave London and set up his new Command Centre at Oxford, the fortress town of Aylesbury was always going to become pivotal to both sides. With an existing castle, courts and jail and the largest population in Buckinghamshire, it was a significant town in its own right, but because of its nearness to the King's redoubt, it was logistically important too.

Right from the beginning the Roundheads seized control, and they never relinquished it. Family and historic influences undoubtedly had a powerful bearing on things. Although he was killed in action early on, Col John Hampden, Cromwell's cousin and 'a true believer' in the new order, had already achieved local hero status after leading a campaign against the Crown's hated 'Ship Money' tax and his friend Col Arthur Goodwin continued to lead Hampden's famous green coats thereafter when he took control of the county's entire force.

Aylesbury's position made it the bridgehead of a Front Line that stretched up to Newport Pagnell, Bedford and Northampton. The town had nailed its colours to the Protestant mast a century earlier when Henry VIII upped its status to county town (over Buckingham) to get himself on the good side of Anne Boleyn's father, the then mayor.

Bulstrode Whitlock, a tough disciplinarian, was first governor of Aylesbury's garrison and a local levy of £200 a week, the most expensive after Newport's, was needed to pay for its upkeep.

Cromwell himself visited the fort many times to encourage his troops and to hear first-hand information about the King's forces from his spies in the field. Henry Marten, a Puritan hard-liner took over the governorship in 1644, but, as with Newport, a regime of marshal law was needed to keep control by 1646 when the restless troops threatened to riot.

Marten was one of the regicides who signed Charles I's death warrant three years later and it was said that he and Cromwell playfully splashed each other with ink during the ceremony. The final controller was Major Gen Charles Fleetwood who was married to one of Cromwell's daughters and also related to the family of Samuel Luke, Newport's governor. Fleetwood was nominally head of the whole republican army at the Restoration in 1660.

The Royalists' strategy

After the loss of the garrison towns in the south Midlands, the Royalists were left with only Banbury, Towcester and Stony Stratford as bases of local command and support for their forces on Front Line activities.

Banbury Castle

Banbury was the Crown's most important stronghold outside of Oxford and an integral element of their operations in the southern Midlands. Heavily walled, gated and moated it was a formidable bastion under the command of Sir William Compton, brother of the Earl of Northampton. It survived a long blockade by more than 3,000 Roundheads in 1644 but succumbed to another siege in 1646 and was sacked.

Towcester

Ancient Roman town also known as *Toster* or *Toxiter* on the London–North Wales highway (Watling Street) at the important junction with the Oxford to Northampton road. After occupation by Prince Rupert's troops in late October 1643, work on building fortifications began immediately. It would have been useful as a forward garrison for the King but quickly became isolated after the loss of Grafton Regis and Rupert's men were 'withdrawn back to bolster the King's defences at Oxford' in January 1644.

Stony Stratford

Established as a field station in late 1643, Stony's enclave was run by the Earl of Cleveland who had family at Toddington. A market town on Watling Street, it was described as 'straggling' and 'very ordinary' (VCH 1927) but popular. A small skirmish there one night in November 1643, when a handful of sentries were killed or wounded was enough to send Cleveland's men retreating back to Oxford. Thereafter it appears to have been an occasional assembling point for Royalist troops.

Other than these locations, the cavaliers were forced to rely on a network of fortified country houses and estates as their supply centres for battle. Although often remote, those places usually had battlements, walls and a moat, and with stockpiles of food and ammunition the plan was that determined defenders should be able to hold out for a number of days until help arrived. One by one they fell to the Roundheads, who then either destroyed them or turned them to their own use. There were several in the 'frontier land' between Newport and Oxford including:

Chicheley Hall, Newport Pagnell

Home of Sir Anthony Chester and his brother John, the Hall was seized early on and turned into an outpost of the garrison with stabling and quarters for the troops. Later burned down.

Grafton House, near Towcester

Bombarded under siege by a combined force from Newport and Northampton and overrun at Christmas 1643, the House was plundered and many prisoners taken including John Digby, son of the Gunpowder Plot conspirator.

Hillesden House, near Buckingham

The home of Sir Alexander Denton, Hillesden captured and plundered by Samuel Luke's troops from Newport in March 1644. Oliver Cromwell himself took part in the assault.

Boarstall

The Denham family's fortified manor house on the Buckinghamshire border north-east of Oxford, and its neighbouring former Royal hunting lodge at Brill, came under siege several times before finally capitulating in 1646.

▸ Chicheley Hall as it is today. Garrison troops used it for stabling and billets

Buckingham

Somewhat inconceivably, Buckingham remained *neutral* throughout the conflict. Indeed, both the King and Oliver Cromwell stayed there at different times (VCH, *A history of the County of Buckingham* vol 3, 1925). Early in 1644, for example, it was reported that Cromwell 'passed several weeks' in the town, while in June, just a few weeks later, the King had more than half his army with him when 9,000 foot and 3,000 horse commandeered the place for four days.

Chapter 4: Inside the fortress

If it were possible for a soldier from Newport Pagnell to revisit the town 360 or so years after being stationed there in the Civil War, he would be amazed to find so much of it unchanged.

True, the town was much smaller then, with fewer houses and a tiny population by comparison, even before the troops moved in to double the numbers, and there was much more open space between the pockets of habitation.

Yet the framework of today's principal roads, the High Street, Silver Street (then known as Marsh Street) and St John's, was already in place. There were bridges as now across the two rivers and more than 30 of the houses and premises he would have been familiar with are still in existence.

Certainly the main roadways were less populated and foreshortened in those days with the bottom of High Street opening out into a grassy place named The Green, St John's being separated from Tickford End and Silver Street dwindling into virtual marshland alongside the river Lovat (then known as the Ouzel). But the basic layout is much the same.

Newport was ideal in many ways as a place to turn into a command centre for military operations and supplies and not just because of its geographical position at the crossing point of two rivers and several important highways. The town itself already possessed a well-established and prosperous infrastructure with bustling markets since the 13th century, a burgeoning trade (fine bone lace-making), 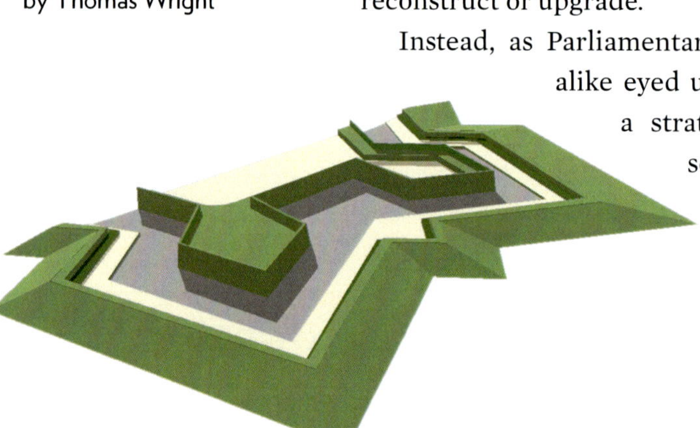 a variety of stores and small businesses, inns and hostelries, and a civil administration which included burgesses (councillors), courts, a gaol and a town bailiff. Unusually for a town of its size and rural position there was even a significant immigrant population of mostly Calvinist Protestants from Europe's Low Countries, Holland and Belgium, who had fled from religious persecution and come to this area because of its sympathy towards non-conformity.

For the military however, the first thing to consider was how to turn the town into a stronghold secure enough to protect its forces and safeguard the local inhabitants. It would not be easy.

Unlike Northampton, Banbury, Bedford and several other places in the region which had existing stone-built fortifications like walls, ramparts and castles, even old and disused ones, Newport had nothing so solid to build onto, reconstruct or upgrade.

Instead, as Parliamentarian and Royalist commanders alike eyed up the town for its potential as a strategic garrison, their thoughts settled on earthwork defences as the answer. In fact, Newport was among many sites in the conflict where earth rather than stone would become the preferred material of choice and engineers capable of designing and building these types of defences were much in demand.

Newport's reputation for fine lace was well established by the 17th century and had already received royal patronage from Elizabeth I and Queen Anne, James I's consort. Cromwell's Puritans discouraged it as flamboyant but Cavaliers and their ladies wore lace trimmings to cuffs, collars, kerchiefs, gloves, hats and even shoes. Source: *Romance of the lace Pillow* by Thomas Wright

The likely defences would have had a *glacis* or man-made slope outside the walls allowing defending troops a clear sight to fire down on attackers still needing to cross a water-filled ditch

46

The benefit of earthworks was that construction of the fortifications could be achieved rapidly and effectively. Basically, the technique was to recycle earth dug from deep ditches around the perimeter by hard-packing it into walls, ramparts and bulwarks with wooden facings (pales or stakes) for added protection and support. The ditches would then be flooded to create a moat both wide and deep and a formidable barrier for any attacker.

The method had been well tried in a number of continental wars (see Peitz, Germany below). There were some big

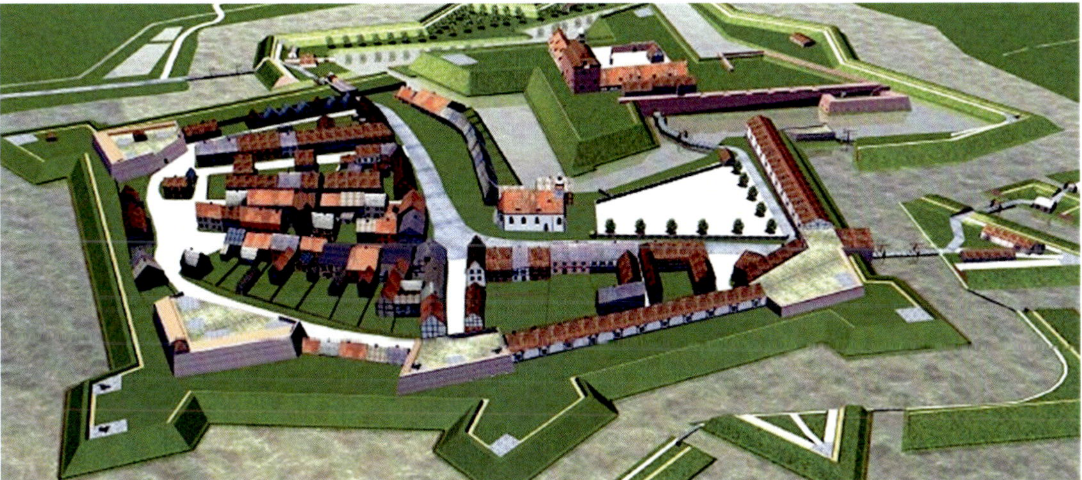

An example 'town inside walls of earth'. This one was at Peitz, in Germany.
© Forderverein für die Museen der Stadt Peitz e.V.

drawbacks, especially in places like Newport where regular river flooding would undermine or even wash away whole sections of the palisades leading to continuous repairs and expense. But in the hurly-burly of those early days of the war it was unlikely that much thought was given to the longer term.

At Newport Pagnell, where the dashing Prince Rupert put Sir Lewis Dyve in control of defence building works during their brief occupation in October 1643, the race to build earthwork fortifications began immediately and much local labour was impressed into the Royalists' attempt to build a fort to house more than a thousand of the King's men with guns and supplies.

They were not long on the job. Military control changed hands within days. Parliament's troopers from London found it abandoned, either by mistake or desertion and Sgt Major Skippon and his officers called in their own experts to finish the task.

They needed, according to records: '300 shovels and spades, 200 pickaxes, 500 wheel-barrows, 400 spars and 1,000 deal boards,' plus, it can be assumed, the services of at least 500 labourers.

Again, because of its importance to rebel plans, the work at Newport was given top priority and the man appointed to head up the construction, Capt Cornelius van den Boom, a Dutch engineer highly skilled in earthwork defences and how to deal with erosion by water, was perfectly qualified.

Composed within a roughly rectangular shape, the Dutchman's plan (see drawing from 1644 on page 50) was to build a shield of earthwork fortifications about 10–12ft high around the town so attackers could be driven off by a combination of fire from the ramparts or by heavier guns and cannon blasting from nine or ten bastions placed strategically around the perimeter.

It was important that land adjacent to the fort should be clear of trees and buildings where an enemy could gather in numbers to mount a sustained attack and here again, the town was well-placed because extensive felling work to provide spars for the palisades had laid waste to large areas of Burgh/ Bury Field, Castle Mead/Meadow, Tickford End and Porters Field which were all unenclosed common lands at that time.

Harnessing his knowledge of floodplain management from Holland, van den Boom used the waters of the River Ouse on the north-west boundary and the Ouzel (Lovat) on the south-east to secure the town with a moat up to 10ft deep and 15ft wide on two sides, and then directed that a ditch be dug out to complete the triangle across the eastern end.

Then he had the ingenious idea of digging sluices from the Ouse across what is known today as Bury Field so the area

▲ Cutaway of a rampart and moat section from van den Boom's plan

could be quickly flooded into a boggy morass which would make any attack from the north-westerly direction virtually impossible.

Inside the fortress, entry or exit along two of the principal roads (north towards Northampton and Leicester and south-east towards London) was across defendable bridges, while access from the third, going east towards Stony Stratford, could only be achieved over a sentry-controlled drawbridge on what is today the Wolverton Road.

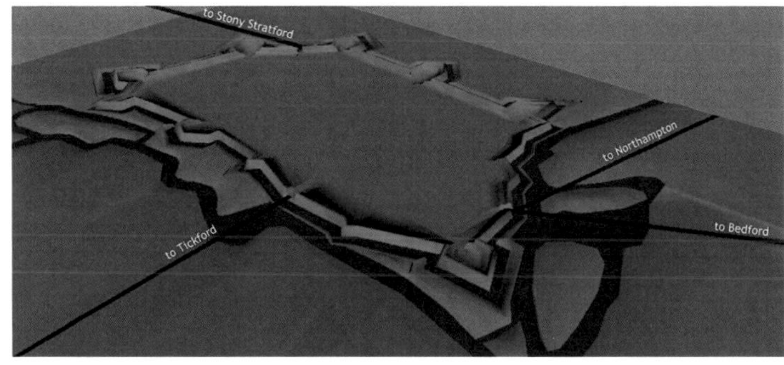

▲ **A computer reconstruction of what the earthwork fortifications may have looked like** – Courtesy of Dominic Goode M.Eng (Bath)

There were two medieval bypasses, one behind the town linking the Bedford Road to Tickford End along a track[18] from Sherington known as 'Thee old road to Newport' and via a washway (ford) across the Ouse east of the ruined Priory, and the other, since Roman times, linking the Stony Stratford road with the Northampton highway via a hamlet based on Kickles Farm beyond Bury Field.

Other points of note on van den Boom's plan were his names for various bastions or bulwarks where buildings were protected, such as 'Tannery' and 'Mill', and the area called the 'Mount' bulwark below the church where a battery of heavy cannon was set out in the apex between the two converging rivers, presumably to engage any enemy forces approaching from the Tickford direction.

The Dutchman's scheme to turn Newport into an impregnable fortress proved so successful that not a single direct attack by Royalist troops during the entire War is recorded. ◑ Indeed, the only incursion made by forces loyal

◑ The nearest probably being Ratcliff's account of the Earl of Cleveland riding from the Royalists' forward station at Stony Stratford to defeat a band of rebels 'within sight of Newport' in July 1643.

---

18 From map dated 1580 in *Fiefs and Fields of a Buckinghamshire village* (AC Chibnall, OUP 1965).

▲   **Map of the fortifications planned for Newport by the Dutch engineer Cornelius van den Boom
dated 1644. The original is in the Bodleian Library at Oxford.**
The Bodleian Libraries, The University of Oxford MS.Top.Bucks.b.6

The River.
The Meadow.
way to Northampton.
way to Olney.
The Meadowe.
The River.
profyl
A Scale of the profyl. Lang 50. Foot.
Cora: van den Boom
Jngenieur Fecit

51

to the King came in the Spring of 1644 when a number of men slipped past the guards and raided Sir Samuel Luke's house in an attempt to assassinate him. More detailed accounts are rare but it is said that he fought them off alone until help arrived.

But such formidable defences came at a huge financial cost. Parliament's edict on December 18, 1643 approved a monthly levy to pay for the complete operation at Newport with the equivalent of £145,000 being immediately set aside for the all-important earthworks. The money was meant to come from the 'three hundreds' of Newport, and proportionate levies on the eight adjacent counties – but it was not guaranteed and very often fell short, leaving Sir Samuel to send out a stream of increasingly desperate letters to his superiors and even, as a last resort, to beg funds from his father.

Van den Boom's fellow Dutchman, Bartholomew Vermuyden, was appointed Quartermaster with responsibility for hiring labour and maintaining supplies and it is clear that hundreds, and sometimes thousands, of civilian workmen were drafted onto the site.

Pay was set at 8 pennies (3.3p) per day for labouring and 48 pennies (20p) per day for a team with a horse and cart and such was the priority given to the garrison's defences that there were instances where workmen were paid before the soldiers.

What Earthworks can be seen today?

Although experts agree that 'substantial bank and ditch defences were constructed around the town' archaeologists have struggled to confirm exactly what was where in Newport and the absence of much preserved evidence is thought to be a possible reason why so little has been written about the important Civil War era in the town's history.

Based on the standard multiplier

The eight counties were Beds, Herts, Northants, Cambs, Suffolk, Norfolk, Hunts and Essex.

Earthwork walls were quick to put up but were also quick to destroy. After the War, Newport's Parliamentary troops were ordered to 'sleight' the fortifications (pull them down) to prevent another enemy making use of them. It is also likely that much of the superstructure was pushed straight into the ditches or moats alongside, and the British weather plus frequent river flooding would have soon washed away any earthwork remains, just as it did in many other locations.

Temporary investigations during modern-day building works or renovations are said to have uncovered traces of 'substantial ditches' or moats in Silver Street, High Street and Mill Street, but experts seem uncertain about much other evidence.

According to the Bucks County Council Heritage Town Assessment[19] the only existing remains are earthworks found in Bury Lawn (on the perimeter of Burgh/Bury Field) and now designated as a Scheduled Ancient Monument. There is also some stonework walling in Bury Field and anecdotal evidence suggests that further stonework may be incorporated into today's Mill House.

Paul Woodfield, Buildings Conservation Officer for Milton Keynes Development Corporation between 1973–1984, concluded that an elevated area in Ousebank Gardens is what remains of the Mount bulwark and that the remnants of a forward battery is in the churchyard. But he asserts: 'Nothing survives within the town.' [20]

As to life within the walls, religious surveys at the time put Newport's resident population at 'towards' 2,000

---

19 *Historic Town Assessment – Newport Pagnell, draft 1*
    (Bucks CC and MKC) – Sept 2010

20 *The last skirmish – Stony Stratford 1644*

if incorporating the hamlets of Tickford, Lathbury and Sherington. By comparison, the town was then roughly the same size as Bedford.

Being an established centre of trade, Newport was quite used to having a large influx of people from local villages on market days, but nothing on the scale of the full complement of Parliamentary forces, about 1,200 foot, 300 cavalry plus camp followers and support services, who would be stationed there officially.

In reality, with many troops frequently out on patrol or away supporting other task forces and campaigns and by utilising temporary pitches at the several large open fields close by, there was rarely a problem of overcrowding in the town.

At one time it is recorded that officers ordered makeshift barracks be built in the middle of the High Street, but evidently the structure was so rickety it soon collapsed.

Instead, billeting of troops at Tickford, Caldecote and Lathbury (where there was also stabling for the cavalry and a jail compound for prisoners) was supplemented by sequestrated quarters at outlying Olney, Hanslope, Castlethorpe, Loughton, Sherington, Chicheley and Linford which brought the added benefit of circling the town with an 'early warning' chain of sentries and patrols.

Inside the garrison[21] the streets were typically of rounded cobblestones and the houses had roofs of slate or thatch with mullioned windows and timbered walls of limestone. Gulleys beside the thoroughfares will have been little more than open sewers.

Remarkably, at least 30 premises and buildings in Newport have survived the three and a half centuries since the Civil

Newport's population today is about 17,000

Villages around Newport Pagnell (original spellings) were then: Sherrington, Chicheley, Little Lynford, Astwood, Bradwell, Bodington, Tykeford, Broughton, Crawley, Tyrringham, Sulbury, Wyllyn, Calcott, Lathbury, Hardmead, Filgrave, Clifton, Goatehurste (Gayhurst), Thornbury, Liscombe, Loughton, Stanton Barry, Kickle or Kickelett and Midleton Keyns – the last of which then consisted of just a handful of houses three miles downstream from Newport on the Ouzel.

---

21 Sources include: *In the footsteps of Bunyan* (Vera Brittain); *History of Newport Pagnell* (Staines); *Historic Town Assessment draft 2010* (NPagnell Hist Soc); *History of Parliament Dec 1643* (VCH 1911); and personal conversations with the author

War and some for far longer than that. Mostly they are along High Street, St John's and Silver Street with another small cluster at Tickford.

An appreciation of the town as it was then (note the A–Z references of significant places) is as follows:

The High Street was then as now where the majority of daily trade took place but first, as the main roadway from the north, it entered over a guarded bridge across the Ouse and began up the hill past a wealthy merchant's house (a) to the ancient church of *St Peter & St Paul* (b) around which so much of life in the fortress revolved.

Opposite and below the church, it is thought that one of at least three weekly markets would have set up in North Square which opened out at the top end of Mill Street beyond the shadow of a number of corn and fulling (cloth-making) mills co-existing beside the river. It seems likely too that a water reservoir for the citizens, filled by hydraulic pump and built by the same Dutch engineers who had masterminded the garrison's defensive earthworks, was also sited in this part of town.

▲ Church Passage leads up to St Peter & St Paul, a focus of religious worship for troops in the town

Meanwhile, back up by the church and casting a look down the wide and cobbled vista of the High Street, there was much activity going on.

On the eastern side stood the imposing *Swan Inn* (c), popular across more than a century as a warm and hospitable stop-over for coachmen and their passengers, while right beside it the dark and business like *Saracens Head,* even older dating from the 15th century and, at this time of the Civil War, the centre of Governor Luke's administration of all matters military and civilian.

▲ **The Swan Hotel (later renamed the Swan Revived after surviving a fire) was a centre of garrison life together with the Saracen's Head which then stood next-door on the High Street's eastern side**
From an old drawing courtesy of the NP Historical Society

Here, like today's local worthies, the guild of burgesses would meet to deal with civic matters affecting the town, and the mayor, treasurer and bailiff, whose job it was amongst other things to keep order in the alehouses, would decide how to ensure safe collection of road tolls and market rents.

Governor Luke would arrive here after the short walk from his adopted home at The Green, down by the brewery (d) with the 16th century *Dolphin Inn* alongside and the north-western defences (e) and (f) behind, to chair the Parliamentarian's local 'committee for the sequestration of estates of delinquents and Papists', ⊙ damning every Royalist and demanding they pay all taxes and tithes or face the threat of having their land or property confiscated.

Across from the *Saracen's Head* and *Swan,* with its popular *Swan Tap* bar at the back, stood The *George* and the ever-welcoming *Wagon & Horses* where George Fox, the pacifist Quaker leader, had based himself for three months during the Spring of 1644 while unsuccessfully haranguing the troops to abandon all thoughts of violence.

No doubt Mr Fox will have also held a view about the town's second and largest market, or 'shambles' as it was called, where the butchers, bakers and tradesmen set up their booths and stalls outside what became known as

⊙ Delinquent was the name given to all Monarchists by the Parliamentary side; Papists were Catholics.

Cannon's Corner (g) with surviving buildings No's. 30 (h) and 38 (i) close by.

Next, heading down St John's Street, our Civil War soldier would have noted the wooden-beamed buildings at No 16 – *Picture This* (j) and *Astons* at No 26 (k) a tiny, timber-framed property with a wooden stair tower that has changed little in more than 300 years, and the ancient stone former vicarage (l) at No. 32.

He would also have heard, only too often, the harrowing cries of pain and anguish from wounded colleagues at the ancient St John's Hospital down the hill near the Tickford Bridge which the Danish Queen Anne, consort of James I, had blessed and re-dedicated during her visit to the town in 1615 (m).

And further, after the bridge guards had allowed him to venture out into Tickford End, he recalled how the family of royal doctor Henry Atkins had become owners of the stately Abbey (n) with its walled deer park and picturesque fishponds and the Priory behind, its ruined archways and broken columns presenting a sharp reminder of King Henry's VIII's seismic break with the Church of Rome a century before.

After retracing his steps across the bridge and back up the hill, our trooper made his turn west into Marsh Street (o) today known as Silver Street, and began to stride out down Newport's winding and, as many believed, most attractive avenue.

Here, at the top end, he would find another 'shambles' (with goods for ladies on this particular day), and then further down a broad selection of stores, inns and emporia on either side including:

No 19.	The Hermitage, a large imposing building from the 17th century (p)
No's 16–18:	two timber-framed cottages, one with an unusual jettied front (q)
No 23:	Lincoln Lodge (r)

No 72: a thatched house that had been here since medieval days (s)

Interestingly, he also glimpsed a short-cut across the little alley of Paggs Court/Chapel Court which would one day allow an outlawed preacher to nip unseen through a huddle of old shelters and barns from a religious meeting house off High Street (t). (see Rev Gibbs sketch file, p104)

And finally, after passing a tannery (u) on the Ousel which produced everything from leather wear to parchment for lace-making, the track began to peter out amidst the nearness of the reed-strewn river. Here was what locals called Marsh End, a misty place of tangled undergrowth and sad willows where the fortress walls ended in a bastion called Bull, and an old thatched house (v) which had stood there since Tudor times, marking the garrison's southern boundary.

▼ **Bury Field, Common land to the north side of town which could be flooded deliberately in the event of an attack**

What buildings have survived?

KEY: Using matching alphabetical identifiers, here is what those building are today plus notes of some landmarks that no longer exist. The list is not exhaustive and complete accuracy is not guaranteed.[22]

High Street

(a) *Royal British Legion* building with north end of churchyard and Ousebank Gardens behind

(b) *St Peter & St Paul* parish church; reconstructed 14th century with tower from 16th.

(c) *Swan Revived Hotel;* the original Swan Inn from 1543 burned down hence today's 'revived' successor

(g) Is the general area in front of the *Cannon* pub

(h) Three-storey whitewashed private house with fine plaster detailing next to the Post Office

(i) *Vanilla* bridal shop. Strikingly attractive double bay building with beams and wattle/daub rendered exterior

---

22 *VCH online; NP Historical Society; Historic Town Assessment – Newport Pagnell, draft 2010;* information given to the author

The Green

n/a Governor Luke was believed to have had his private quarters here

(d)   The town's brewery was here – probably on the site of today's *Boots/Health Centre* – with The *Dolphin Inn* dating from the 16th century alongside

(e, f) Evidence found of 'defensive ditches' during excavations for Tankard Close and behind the police station

St John's Street

(j)   *Picture This* art shop; stone, brick and timber building, possibly former barn

(k)   *Astons* estate agency; narrow three-storey brick and timber construction

(l)   *The Old Vicarage* (and curate's house); substantial private residence, parts dating from 1560

     (m) *St John's Hospital;* exact site unknown but beam dated 1615 in nearby almshouse states: *'All you good Christians that here do pass by, give something to those poor people that in St John's hospital do lie'.* Re-founded by Queen Anne of Denmark, consort of James I, during visit to the town.

Tickford End

(n) *Tickford Abbey;* today a residential care home with waste ground on the nearby deer park and gardens site awaiting development

(o) Today's Silver (was Marsh) Street

(p) *The Hermitage* (no 19); substantial double chimney brick and tile residence

◀ **A dedication to Queen Anne is still visible on this gable end near Tickford Bridge**

(q)   *No's 16 & 18;* adjacent pair of timber-framed cottages; attractive facia of brick and beam, one with jettied construct.

(r)   *Lincoln House* and *Lincoln Lodge;* large whitewashed property, probably former merchant's residence, now split into two homes

(s)   A thatched cottage was said to have stood here (No 72) in Civil War times. Today, the site has been comprehensively developed.

(t)   *Paggs Court* and *Chapel Court;* offered covert backyard exits into Marsh Street from the meeting house and barns where today's *United Reformed Church* stands. The minister Rev John Gibbs held services here in William Smyth's barn from 1660. An original stone and pebble pathway with drainage is a feature at Paggs Court.

Marsh End

(u)   Tannery then producing leatherwear and parchment for the lacemakers was on the Ousel (Lovat) near today's *Cowley Parchment Works* on Caldecote Street.

(v)   *Lovat Crest;* thatched house with black beam and whitewash detailing believed to be Tudor and among the town's oldest surviving structures

Military activity inside the fortress

The clothes they wore

Military life at Newport was never more varied and colourful than during its first three years as a fortified garrison.

With hundreds of soldiers in the place there was constant activity with drills and practising (especially for new recruits enlisted during 1644 including the teenage John Bunyan – see Chapter 6), patrols and sentry duties and military policing.

Marauding parties were sent out into 'the field' to search for food, supplies, materials and livestock; platoons regularly went off to skirmish with Royalist soldiers in the locality; and larger detachments were dispatched on assignments or to join with forces from other areas for major battles and confrontations.

In the early days of the conflict, when it was difficult to tell friend from foe, coloured sashes were often used for identification. Later, some on the Parliamentarian side were recognisable by their coloured coats and trimmings like the 'Green and Golds' of the so-called London Trained Bands who came up from the capital to occupy Newport Pagnell, but most of the others, and especially conscripts and volunteers, wore a motley collection of clothing. For troopers it consisted of a plain brown doublet and coat, short breeches, shirt, long cotton stockings, laced shoes and a large felt hat or knitted 'monmouth' cap, and for officers, armoured breast plates, knee breeches, long leather boots and high plumed hats.[23]

Typically, a musketeer or foot soldier would carry a short flintlock with leather bandolier over his shoulder containing powder and shot, pikemen would present a formidable shield during battle with their 15ft long staves, and dragoons picked for their superior fighting skills would need to have

---

23 Additional information from Vera Brittain's book *In the steps of Bunyan*

themselves suitably dressed for fighting on foot one day and on horseback the next. 

Sometimes having no recognisable uniform was also an advantage, especially for the 'army' of clandestine spies and informers who came constantly to and from Newport's garrison with vital information for Governor Luke.

Sir Samuel was a brilliant scoutmaster, not a leader of today's boy scouts but military scouts who were the eyes and ears of the Parliamentarian army. Because the fort was on the front line and there were major highways passing nearby it was imperative to know as quickly and accurately as possible where the enemy troops were and when they had started, or, better still, when they were *thinking* of starting to move.

Governor Luke concentrated on the no man's land between Newport and the King's base at Oxford, sending and receiving scores of letters and messages every day and particularly when a major battle or engagement was brewing. Some said his intelligence network was so good he knew what the Royalists were going to do, before they knew themselves.

Because of Luke's scoutmaster skills at Newport, Cromwell always gave a high priority to the value of 'inside' information and later, in 1653 when his trusty old friend had long since retired,Cromwell appointed the shrewd and clever John Thurloe as his director of spying and intelligence.

Cromwell's officers did not wear their famous red coats until after the New Model Army was formed in 1645.

▶ **A typical musketeer with flintlock and bandolier**
Illustration by Christian Lilt

▲ Modern redcoat musketeers
stage a re-enactment

The guns they fired

Larger pieces of artillery were positioned on the bulwarks to fend off attack or were standing ready to accompany outgoing troops on major assignments.

Drake artillery pieces could fire 6lb shots from the ramparts while greater firepower was available from *Culverin* or *demi-Culverins* blasting 15lb and 9lb balls respectively for up to 1 ½ miles from battery emplacements like the one behind Newport's parish church.

Smaller artillery was certainly taken out by garrison men on patrol or on assignment when they had a particular target in prospect. *Minions,* a light field gun that could send 4lb shot for nearly a mile, was a useful anti-personnel weapon followed up with *fireballs, mortars* and early *hand-grenades.*

On the other hand, if a siege was likely, they would have taken the superior *Cannons,* cumbersome to pull with a horse and crew, but with 47lb shot capable of knocking large holes in the thickest walls and buildings.

Leading by example

Even if they had other specialities, Parliament's senior officers at Newport Pagnell were required to lead by example by heading up their own divisions of troops. Cornelius van den Boom, the Dutch engineer, had a troop of foot soldiers as did his Dutch colleague Bartholomew Vermuyden, the Quartermaster. Sir Samuel Luke, the Governor, frequently went out with his men on dangerous assignments and personally commanded a troop of cavalry.

Chapter 5: Action stations

Prince Rupert, the King's flamboyant nephew, swore revenge after learning of the catastrophic blunder which handed back control of Newport Pagnell to the Parliamentary side, after less than a fortnight, in October 1643.

With the Civil War little more than a year old it had become obvious to him, just as it was to the senior strategists of both sides, that the axis of Northampton, Newport Pagnell, Bedford and Aylesbury would be strategically vital to control the supply lines between East Anglia, where Parliament's military support was strongest and London where its political power was concentrated.

Not since the Danes and Saxons divided up the kingdom along the line of the Ouse had this 'middle England' become such an important battleground and army leaders on both sides realised, quite rightly as it turned out that this would be where, in the first phase at least, the Civil War would be won or lost.

Now, after the bungle at Newport, Parliament's forces had control of all four of those important towns.

Prince Rupert, the King's most senior general and a leader who inspired his men by personal example, refused to accept the situation. He argued that a swift response was essential, before the Parliamentarians consolidated themselves, and within days he was back 'on the patch' trying to wrest back control.

Informants from Towcester who heard that the Prince was calling up a large number of troops were in no doubt about what was planned. 'They give it out that they will have Newport againe whatever it cost them, begging pardon for my boldness' wrote one officer to the Earl of Essex, who was in charge of the Parliamentarian army.[24] The warning came true soon enough.

The Battle of Olney Bridge

Just a month before, when Prince Rupert's cavalry had tested the defences of the fortified castle of Northampton, they had been driven off by a withering hail of heavy cannon fire, so he chose not to make that his first target this time around.

Instead, early on November 4, a crisp Saturday morning, the Prince determined to make a surprise assault on Newport from the north-east through Olney, in other words, using a phrase he was as yet most reluctant to accept, it was to be 'an attack from behind enemy lines'.

Being little more than a fortnight since Newport's re-occupation by Parliament's troops no doubt he thought that Olney, a small town on the Ouse three miles or so distant from it, would be clear of his enemy. But he was wrong.

Already the town had become a sizeable billet for troops from the Newport garrison and although it was very early in the morning, sentries and look-outs were wide awake and the officer in charge, Colonel Edmund Harvey, was well up to the challenge that was about to confront him.

The outcome became forever known locally as *The Battle of Olney Bridge*. It was the first action in the area with significant violence and casualty lists and it would mark the start of a succession of lethal confrontations in the vicinity over the

---

24 *History & Antiquities*, Ratcliff ibid p58–59

The 'Battle of Olney' bridge was built in 1619 to improve an existing structure. This photo, kindly provided by the Cowper & Newton museum, shows a successor bridge known as the Old Duchy. The present Iron construction dates from 1894. A number of Civil War skulls and swords from those who perished at the bridge are also held at the museum.

next six months as the Front Line of the great conflict was tested and established.

As so often with reports of events in the Civil War, both sides gave very different accounts of what took place and the spreading of news, mainly by handbills and propaganda sheets, was frequently inaccurate, out of date or incomplete.

Nonetheless what seemed to have happened at Olney was that Rupert's substantial force, consisting of 'several regiments of cavalry, 400 dragoons and 200 musketeers' stormed quickly through the town, brushing aside all resistance from the Roundheads. It was said that this took them only 15 minutes, but that was still enough time for the rest of Colonel Harvey's defenders to fall back to the bridge where they took up positions to make a stand, barred the route onward to Newport and crucially, dispatched riders urgently seeking reinforcements from the garrisons there and at Northampton. 'An orderly retreat,' recorded the Parliamentarian chronicler.

In the action, and not for the first time, Olney's narrow bridge over the Ouse became a great equalizer as it funnelled Prince Rupert's troops and enabled Col Harvey's men to pour their musket fire into the bottleneck. Most importantly too, it bought them time, time to hold out for those reinforcements

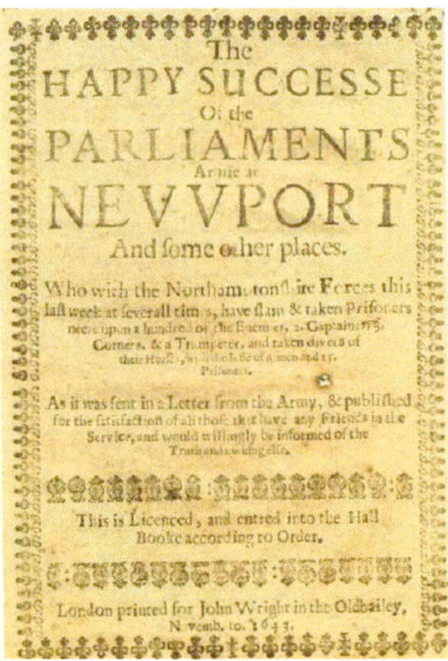

Happy successes at Newport, declared the poster

and so, when it became clear to Prince Rupert that he was not going to win the fight before the superior numbers arrived, he called his men together and wheeled them away on the long route around to his nearest 'friendly' garrison at Towcester.

'A tactical withdrawal,' declared the Royalists' handbill.

Subsequent claims over casualty numbers only continued the confusion. '60 of their men killed, 40 captured and 120 horses dead or injured,' boasted the War's Royal diarist, yet handbills for the Parliamentary side were soon proclaiming: '*A happy success of the Parliament's army at Newport and some other places ... after slaying and taking prisoner neare upon a hundred of the enemie,*' while their own losses had been just six dead and 15 taken prisoner, it contended.

Siege of Grafton Regis

There were many good reasons for the anti-monarchists to choose the emblematic Grafton Regis as their next local target.

For a start, the sprawling Crown estate represented the recent royals' indulgent lifestyle of hunting, profligacy and extravagant entertaining while they taxed the country beyond reason to fill their empty coffers.

Then there was its proximity to the newly-established Front Line. At Hanslope, closest point to Newport at just a handful of miles from the edge of the 1,000-acre Grafton estate, there would be little time to detect or deter an attack from that direction on the garrison town, it was argued.

Meanwhile, within the new walls of the fortress, the battle-hardened men of the Green and Gold 'bands' from London who had marched up from the capital to win it back for their cause just two months ago, were now growing restless from inactivity. Digging moats and fortifying the town with walls and earthworks was one thing, but these tough troops under their gritty commander Major Gen Philip Skippon were 'running hot' for another contest.

Samuel Luke, not yet in charge of the Newport garrison but already a very significant part of its daily life, would surely have felt the need for revenge to be exacted in anticipation of an attack on the estate.

His expanding collection of field scouts, the network of spies for which he would ultimately earn a place among the Parliamentarians' most enduring legends, was already reporting that Col. Sir John Digby, son of the Gunpowder Plotter Sir Everard Digby, had been put in charge at Grafton where he had spent the last

▲ **Grafton Manor today is a care home**

month throwing up defences around Henry VIII's famous old hunting lodge-cum-mansion and increasing the number of its defenders.

What sweet irony Luke and the others must have thought, to be given the opportunity of blowing up the son of the traitor who had wanted to blast Parliament to smithereens not 40 years before.

In their now-traditional *mode d'employ,* the forces from Newport planned to gather an overwhelming number of troops for the anticipated siege of Grafton.

It was December 21 1643, less than a week before Christmas, and the weather was at its most foul with heavy snow and roaring winds that whipped flurries into the soldiers' faces and chilled the poorly-clothed men to their bones. But the decision to launch an assault had been made, the die was cast and there was no turning back.

Over at Grafton, Sir Samuel's sources of intelligence were telling him that members of the Crane family, new part-owners of the estate after the desperate Royals had sought to raise funds from its sale, were among fewer than 450 or so unsuspecting officers and men ensconced behind the thick walls of the main house and church.

Against them, on that bitter mid-Winter morning, 1,000 infantrymen from the Green and Golds of London now marched out of Newport with four guns in tow on their way to a rendezvous with 1,400 'cavalry and foot' selected from the Regiment of Horse at Northampton and various other centres in the south Midlands and another 1,000 troops from the Earl of Manchester's Eastern Association with four more artillery pieces. In other words, a 'small army' of almost 3,500 troops to confront the 450 at Grafton. It said a great deal about how much the Parliamentarians wanted to crush all resistance at the Royal redoubt.

Day One of the siege (Friday, December 22)
At first all went well for the defenders of Grafton. Pasture and open fields on three sides of the grand mansion offered little cover for the approaching troops of Parliament and from their vantage point high on the hilltop it was easy for Sir John Digby's men to keep their attackers at a distance using long-range muskets and heavyweight cannon.

Day Two
Forces from the Eastern Association of armed bands who led the previous day's initial assault were sent to forage for food and supplies from surrounding villages while Newport Pagnell's tough Green and Golds took on the weather and today's attacking role.

Again they failed to winkle out Digby's men from behind the thick-walled defences in the house or up the tower of the nearby church and, seeking a solution that would bring the attack to a more rapid conclusion, Col. Whetham dispatched a troop of his men to fetch heavier artillery from Northampton and others to throw up huts and shelters so there was at least some protection from the appalling weather.

Day Three (Christmas Eve)

The four big Saker pieces of artillery dragged across from Northampton soon did their work. Drawn up about 300 yards from their target the guns were beyond the range of the defenders' artillery but able to reach it themselves with their heavier firepower. And as the bigger cannon balls began to smash through the mansion's reinforced roof, the result became inevitable.

By 2 o'clock the message came out: 'Sir John wants to parley...' and just two hours later, with safe passage guaranteed to the Crane family and a huddle of priests and non-combatants, the commander had offered up the house and his men to Major Gen Skippon in unconditional surrender.

Remarkably, the Parliamentary forces said they had lost fewer than 20 dead and 10 wounded in the three-day encounter while another nine had died in an accident when barrels of powder they were guarding exploded. No figures were recorded for dead and wounded among the King's supporters but about 300 prisoners, including a number of officers and Digby 🔍 himself, were marched away to Newport to spend Christmas night there in jail at Lathbury.

Inside the house, despite the heavy bombardment it had taken, Skippon's victorious men now found 'goods, plate and money amounting to a value of many thousands of £s' as they plundered the former Royal palace for what they regarded as legitimate spoils of war.

> *'So we marched with our prisoners towards Newport, very weary by reason of the foulness of the weather, the deepnesse of the way, but praised be God we got safely thither, where we now lye expecting relief everyday, that we may come and rest ourselves.*
>
> *I thank God that neither myselfe, nor any of my souldiers, are hurt, nor not one of our Regiment slaine, notwithstanding we were in great danger and hazard'*
>
> –W.B., Newport Pannel, 25 December 1643

▲ Back safely from Grafton thank God, wrote 'WB' on Christmas Day

🔍 Digby was later taken under guard to the Tower in London where he was subsequently 'swapped' for a high-ranking Parliamentary officer who had also been captured (see also Digby's sketch file on page 24).

Finally, after a Christmas night of some revelry, the mansion was put to the torch next morning and burned to the ground together with all the weather huts and shelters.

Skippon's men from London, jubilant over what they had achieved, were now all for marching onto Towcester where they fancied another fight against the garrison there. But their Major General dissuaded them, arguing they were too tired and the weather too bad.

It was later revealed that Prince Rupert had set out with a large detachment from Oxford on Christmas Eve with the aim of relieving the siege at Grafton, but he had turned back after Royalist scouts told him he was already too late.

Sacking of Hillesden House

The downfall of Hillesden House, another of the 'warm nests' of fortified country estates, as the Parliamentary commanders called them, arrived on March 4/5 of 1644. And Oliver Cromwell himself took part.

The strongly-built mansion standing in an elevated position on a ridge a few miles from Buckingham, had been home to Sir Alexander Denton's family for 200 years.

Some months before, several hundred local labourers had been impressed to dig gun emplacements into the ridge so the Royalist artillerymen could fend off any attacks and with about 170 troops inside, plus 40 or so officers and cavalrymen, it was never going to be easy for the Roundheads to take.

Fortunately for them Sir Alexander, who colleagues described as gentle and affectionate and not perhaps the most ferocious of adversaries, was most concerned about the safety

With Grafton lost, Rupert decided to pull his troops back from Towcester to Banbury in the following month. Large sections of the land at Grafton were sequestrated after the siege in 1644 and sold to London merchants to raise money for Parliament's war chest. What's left of the Manor is today a residential care centre for the mentally ill.

of his relatives. A devoted family man, he had his son John inside plus several of his sisters, daughters and nieces.

Outside meanwhile and with their usual tactic of presenting overwhelming numbers, Sir Samuel Luke had arrived with a large force from Newport and he linked up with a certain Oliver Cromwell, who was then just a Colonel but already rising rapidly in the Parliamentary ranks, at the head of a powerful regiment of cavalry from Aylesbury.

Between them the combined forces mustered no fewer than 2,000 men ready to attack the great house and sure enough the assault did not last long.

The military defenders led by local man Col. William Smith gave up the unequal struggle with the loss of about 40 men, some of whom perished among the battlements of the medieval church of All Saints nearby, while Sir Alexander was soon taken captive together with his sisters and daughters and the church priest Rev Oakeley.

The next day, the grand old house was looted and raised to the ground by Samuel Luke's victorious men and Denton and Smith were marched off to Lathbury and then to the Tower where Denton died next New Year's Day from a fever or, as his family suggested, from a broken heart, aged just 48.

During that year he had lost his house, his son John would be killed in action, and Margaret, one of his daughters, would marry a Roundhead officer she met after the destruction of her family's home.

Conversely, as if having proved his ability to Colonel Cromwell during this latest action at Hillesden, Samuel Luke was officially put in charge of the garrison at Newport.

Rumours persisted locally that about 30 of the King's troopers were killed after they surrendered at Hillesden and that women and children 'had their clothes torn off their backs,' by their captors. But these alleged atrocities were never proved and the story may have been put around as false propaganda.

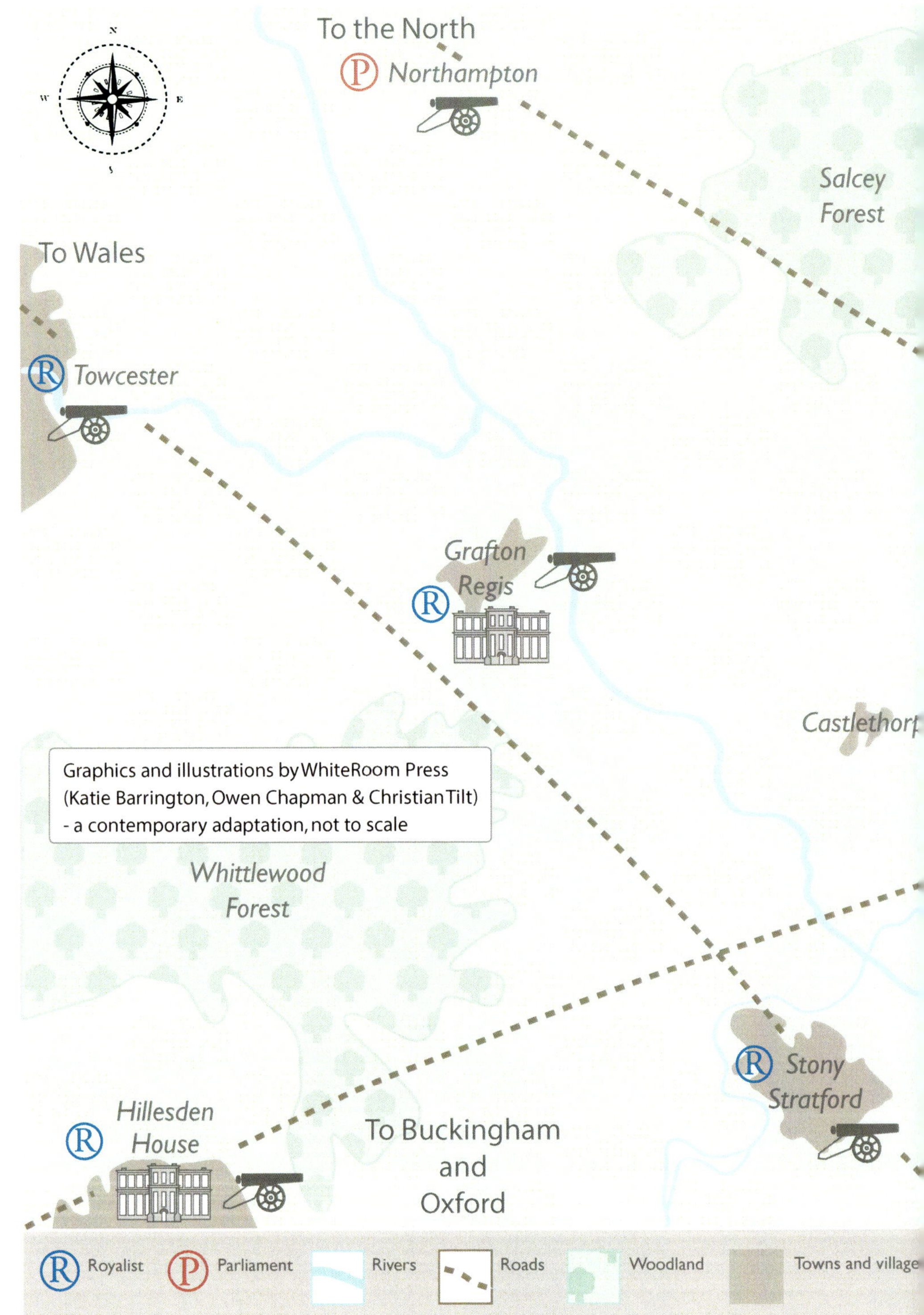
To the North
P Northampton
Salcey Forest
To Wales
R Towcester
Grafton Regis
R
Castlethorp
Graphics and illustrations by WhiteRoom Press
(Katie Barrington, Owen Chapman & Christian Tilt)
- a contemporary adaptation, not to scale
Whittlewood Forest
R Stony Stratford
Hillesden House
R
To Buckingham and Oxford
R Royalist
P Parliament
Rivers
Roads
Woodland
Towns and village

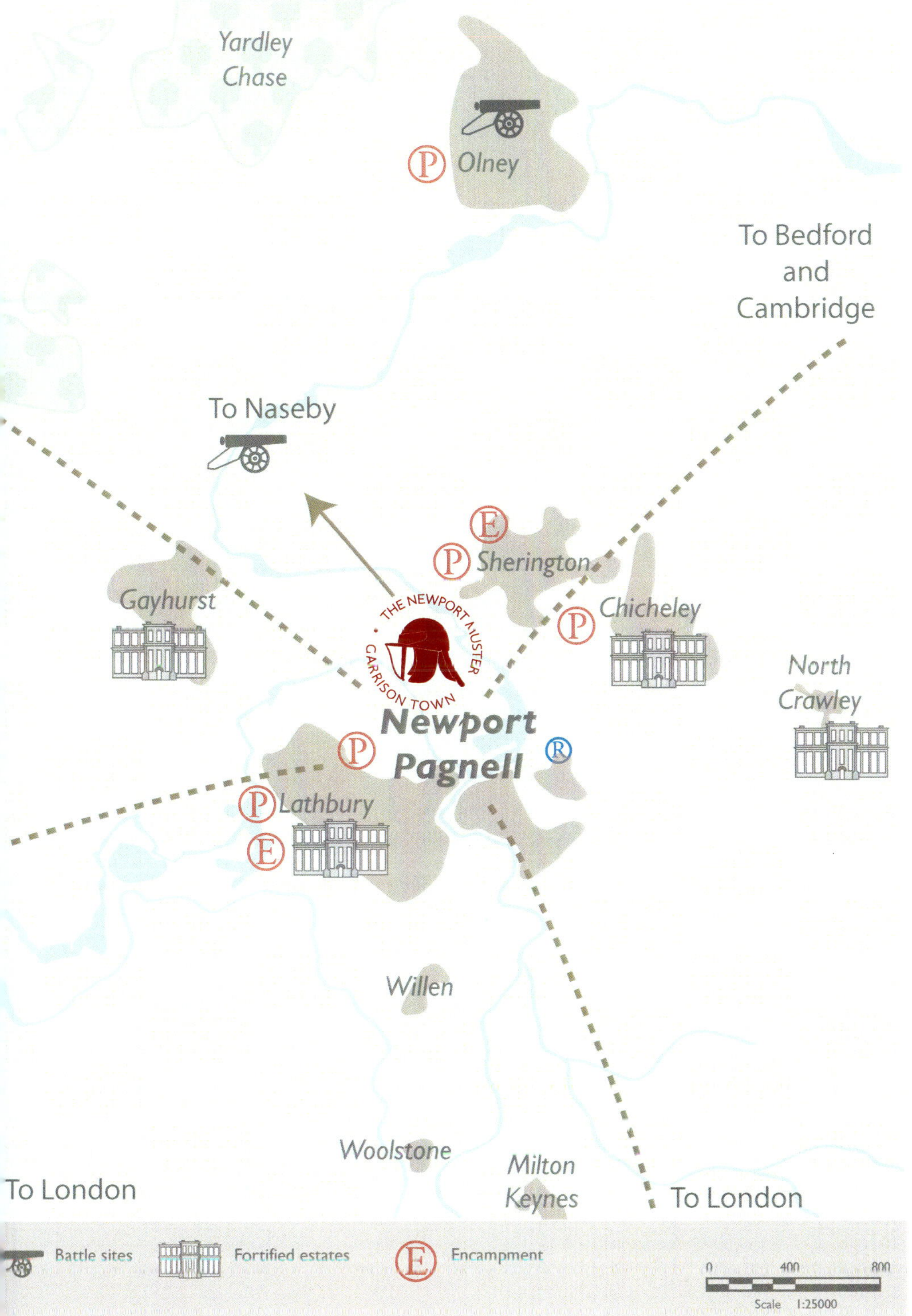

Yardley Chase
Olney
To Bedford and Cambridge
To Naseby
Sherington
Gayhurst
Chicheley
North Crawley
THE NEWPORT MUSTER
GARRISON TOWN
Newport Pagnell
Lathbury
Willen
Woolstone
Milton Keynes
To London
To London
Battle sites
Fortified estates
Encampment
0   400   800
Scale   1:25000

Cromwell's son was his joy

Historians have debated inconclusively over whether Colonel Cromwell's son Oliver junior might have been wounded in the Hillesden action and died subsequently from his wounds.

Young Oliver, who is recorded as dying in the second week of March 1644, just a few days after Hillesden, was serving at Newport Pagnell and could well have been among the large contingent that went there to join his father in laying down the siege.

Officially he is said to have died from camp fever (ie typhoid or smallpox), but it seems possible this could have been manufactured to avoid the negative propaganda of death from a Royalist's bullet.

Oliver, who was only 21, became Colonel Cromwell's oldest surviving son when his brother Robert died at 18 while away at school. It appears probable that his father proposed the posting to Newport because of the high importance with which he considered the garrison there. As Captain Cromwell, a cornet, Oliver junior carried the colours for Troop Eight of the Earl of Bedford's Horse regiment.

Legend locally suggests that for security reasons he was billeted at a sequestrated house in Sherington, a few miles outside Newport and that he may have been buried there in an unmarked grave.

In the *Parliament Scout* of March 15–22 of 1644 it was reported: 'Col Cromwell is gone with his forces to Stony Stratford and Brickhill and begins to increase in power. He hath lost his eldest son at Newport, a civil young gentleman and the joy of his father.'

Coincidentally, or perhaps not, Colonel Cromwell would be back at Sherington little more than a year later when, as head of the New Model Army, he arrived to command a gathering of at least 10,000 troops on the eve of the Battle of Naseby, which effectively decided the Civil War in Parliament's favour.

Whether Col. Cromwell deliberately pressed for the army's rendezvous at Sherington as a personal tribute to his beloved son is still an open question.

Chapter 6: Naseby, Sodom and Gomorrah

Ironically, Governor Luke admitted to being in greatest fear for his garrison's safety in the days leading up to Naseby, the biggest battle of the Civil War.

One after another, his scouts and spies had been bringing messages back in that fateful first week of June 1645 telling him that significant numbers of Cavalier troops were massing with the apparent intent of converging on the Front Line.

His first conclusion was that the Royalists were gathering to launch a major assault on his Newport Pagnell fortress, so long prized by the King and his Commander Prince Rupert, and with troop numbers low he feared the town might be swiftly overrun.

'How ill we are provided,' he wrote in one message courier'd to a fellow officer.[25] 'You cannot but know [that] our horse and men being commanded away and we, not six hundred foot [infantrymen] left in the town. I desire you… to haste hither what men you can, for we have need of two thousand men to man these works.'

---

25 Ratcliff ibid p229 quoting Luke's *Letterbook*

And to another who had recently received troops on secondment from the Newport garrison:[26] 'His Majesty is at [Market] Harborough and his march is intended for this place, therefore I beseech you – let the foot belonging to this garrison be sent home with all speed and, if you can spare us any more, they will be most acceptable for we shall want above a thousand men to man our works.'

However, as the hours passed slowly by, the incoming information from his network of scouts pointed increasingly towards a proposition that the Royal forces were returning from a successful encounter at Leicester and heading for the area around Daventry in south Northamptonshire. When Luke relayed this in a flurry of dispatches to his High Command, the answer came that all available Parliamentary troops should make their way to Newport, and to rendezvous in readiness for battle rather than as reinforcements for the garrison there.

▲ **Redcoats in a re-enactment of the Naseby battle**

That rendezvous spot was to be the hill at Sherington. And what a gathering it was! Over the next few days the air around the unpretentious little village on the outskirts of Newport was thick with the sounds of horses, men and equipment as Lord Fairfax, now commanding the army in place of Essex, led his men in from an operation at Oxford, Capt Charles O'Hara arrived with troops from Hertfordshire, several regiments of foot and horse came in from the Eastern Counties and, to a thunderous cheer, Oliver Cromwell himself rode in at the head of 600 cavalrymen from his famous Ironsides regiment.

All told, by the night of June 7, it was estimated that more than 10,000 men, horses, guns and equipment were camped

26 Ratcliff ibid p229 quoting Luke's *Letterbook*

in Bancroft Field, a space of 100 acres and more between the old Rectory and Manor House.

With shelter at a premium some even commandeered the parish church. More than half of the substantial Parliamentary army had now descended on the unprepared villagers and although they had seen some unusual comings and goings during the course of the war, there was never anything like this.

> **NOTE:** Observers studying army tactics during the war have long wondered why Sherington was selected as the rendezvous site for the majority of the New Model Army on the eve of Naseby. Geographically, the village was judged an excellent place to congregate close to where the King's forces were massing and it was only a mile or so from the Newport fortress with its ready stocks of food and equipment. But some wonder if there was more symbolism to it than that? Historians point out that measured 'as the crow flies' Sherington was exactly mid-way between Oxford and Cambridge, the centres of great significance to either side. And then there was the personal appeal to Cromwell himself of being able to visit the grave of a beloved son before setting out on this most important battle of the war.

In the evening, Cromwell took a detachment down to the garrison where Governor Luke, now quite relieved and rejoicing after his mistaken fears of attack in the previous few days, was ensuring that every scrap of food and supplies would be taken up to the army on the hill.

Accounts of the Commander's visit say that Cromwell was honoured with a full 'peal of ordnance' (a salute of cannon fire) and a tour of the fortress before sharing a meal and wine with the diminutive Governor, probably at his home on The Green. He refused all invitations to sleep within the fortress,

Exact location still unknown per author's inquiries

it was said, preferring instead to ride back up to his men in their bivouac.

At first light next day, sending as many men from his under-strength garrison as he could spare (with John Bunyan among them[27]), Luke must have been able to see the long lines of troops marching up the road to Northampton where they would gather yet more men on the journey towards Naseby and the forthcoming battle.

This time, remembering how his own men had walked into the Newport garrison virtually unopposed back in October 1643, Luke was careful to hold back enough troops to keep the town secure. And as Cromwell himself reminded him, there would be important tasks to organise jointly with the Northampton fortress, like treating injured comrades returning from the battleground.

He also anticipated, quite rightly, that after the conflict between Brixworth and Market Harborough about 30 miles from Newport there would be thousands of Royalist prisoners and stragglers to round-up from the fields and hedgerows of the south Midlands.

Estimates of numbers taking part in the Naseby battle vary greatly but it was generally thought that Parliament mustered between 13,000 and 15,000 men and the Royalists 7,000 to 10,000. By any calculation it was clear that in what had become their standard strategy, the Roundheads had made certain of heavily outnumbering their opposition, on this day by 3 to 2 or even 2 to 1.

At the outset a heavy fog that led to more bloody hand-to-hand fighting than in previous conflicts, left both sides somewhat disorientated, but once the fog cleared it soon became apparent who would win. The battle lasted for not much more than a single morning and in that time the main army of King Charles and his chief general Prince Rupert was so savaged and decimated that it would never recover.

---

27 *The History of Newport Pagnell*, Staines

Oliver Cromwell, now Number Two in the Parliamentary chain of command to Lord Fairfax, won acclaim for the way he led six regiments of cavalry on one wing. Historians generally agree that prior to the contest, months of re-training the Roundheads' disparate troops, individual bands and groups of militia into the New Model Army as a far more proficient fighting force with consistent standards of leadership, discipline and even battledress (the famous red coats), was the most important factor in their success.

Above all, it was also a complete vindication of the campaign by Cromwell and his principal training officer, the newly-promoted Major Gen Philip Skippon, the same doughty soldier who had secured Newport Pagnell during those first, all-important months in late 1643, that the time had come for re-focusing the Parliamentary troops into a hard-edged and far more proficient force.

For the Royalists Prince Rupert and his brother Prince Maurice succeeded in holding their ground for a time with their Bluecoat cavalry, but being outflanked and badly outnumbered it was not long before the King's main force was routed and all resistance broken.

Victory at Naseby did not come without cost to the Roundheads. Major Gen Skippon, whose pike and musket men had held the centre of the New Model Army's formation, received a serious musket wound which kept him out of action for many months

Another successful adoption was Cromwell's demand that all officers had to re-apply for their own posts. This had the effect of re-assessing everyone's abilities and led to the weeding out of incompetent leaders and 'lame ducks'.

▸ Illustration by Christian Tilt

and Commissary-General Henry Ireton, Cromwell's Number Two in charge of the cavalry, was also wounded and taken prisoner.

Nonetheless, in the final tally, with between 1,000 and 1,500 Cavaliers killed and wounded, 4,500 men rounded up as prisoners and large quantities of equipment destroyed or captured, compared with the Parliamentarians suffering fewer than 500–700 killed and wounded, it was clear to everyone which side had won an outstanding victory.

For quite some time after Naseby there was much to attend to in the garrisons at Newport and Northampton.

Their joint operation of sending out patrols to round up defeated and dishevelled Cavaliers fleeing from the battle had paid great dividends. At Northampton it was reported that four wagons heavily loaded with abandoned guns and weapons were brought back to the fort along with 600 captured stragglers, while at Newport the numbers were even larger. More than three thousand were held as prisoners with many being put into the hastily extended prison compound at Lathbury while the rest, and especially those with officer rank, were marched down to London where the most important of them were dispatched to the Tower.

At the Newport fortress, there were many long nights of great celebration following the famous victory, but for Governor Luke it was time to put a plan for his own future into action.

At the end of that month of June and turning aside many attempts to dissuade him, he stood down with the aim of mounting a legal campaign to win back a huge amount in unpaid wages.

Besides being Governor of the fortress Sir Samuel also held the ranks of a Colonel of Foot and Captain of Horse, but virtually from the outset, and despite continuous urging from the House, contributions from other counties and committees had often fallen short of what was needed to pay his wages and those of his men,[28] and many times he had had to borrow from his father Oliver.

Sir Samuel had already been persuaded to stay in post longer than he wanted but now, with Naseby over and being as sure as he could be that the King's army would never recover, he determined to step down from his command of Newport and began instead a legal claim to recover about £4,500 (or c.£600,000 in today's terms[29]) in outstanding back-pay.

Eventually, it was a struggle he would win after a two-year fight through the courts. But even as he prepared to leave the garrison for his new life, Governor Luke, a highly religious man and strict disciplinarian, feared his men would soon be engulfed other in problems that had their origin off the battlefield.

He had first become aware of the dangers of 'a moral decay' in the spring of that Naseby year of 1645.

After capturing the garrison, control of the Newport area had been consolidated with a string of successes at Olney, Grafton, Hillesden and elsewhere but after the excitement of those victories, the men found their time being spent only on less demanding tasks like patrols and security duties, on missions to support other garrisons or field operations elsewhere. Until the Battle of Naseby, there had been little in the way of serious action for the best part of a year and for

---

28 In Cromwell's army, soldiers' daily wages were typically: Colonel 45/- (£2.25); Captain 15/- (75p); Lieut. 4/- (20p); Ensign 3/- (15p); Gunner 2/- (10p) and Corporal 1/- (5p). These rates compared very favourably with a labourer who could earn 8d (3.3p) per day and a horse & cart with team that would cost 20p per day. But with wages constantly in arrears, the Government frequently issued IoUs instead of cash. The troops had no faith in them however, and they could be bought for as little as 8p in the £1- or a discount of 92 per cent!

29 eg x145 ibid

fighting men who had tasted the adrenaline of battle, garrison life had become tedious and frustrating.

Instead, with time on their hands and being young and fit the men grew increasingly boisterous and sought to amuse themselves with the pleasures and thrills of an altogether more earthy kind.

Governor Luke was already complaining about the lifestyle and lax morals of some of his men in correspondence to fellow officers in the months before Naseby. *'Impiety is growne to such a height in this town that myne eyes can no longer indure the sight of it nor myne ears the hearing,'* he wrote to Cornelius Holland in March 1645. *'Truely Sir... if I stay here I must have liberty to free the town of them least God in his wrath deale with us as hee did with Sodom and Gomorrah.'*

In particular, he complained that adultery was rife and there were more than a few women *'delivered of children'* without knowing who the father was. There was fighting, gambling, drunkenness and general lawlessness among the many inns and taverns of a town that had always possessed more of them than most, as a consequence of its frequent market days and as a stopover for coach travellers.

In the main Sir Samuel blamed conscripted recruits like Bunyan rather than his regular troopers for much of the decadence, but he admitted that the poor facilities, constant lack of pay and even basic clothing, was a drain on morale that left his men *'demoralised and liable to mutiny'*.

NOTE: John Bunyan became familiar with the taverns and brothels (of the town), wrote Vera Brittain in her book *In the Steps of Bunyan* (p89). 'Now an adult, he shared with his contemporaries the normal impulses of young male adulthood. The tankard and dice-box no longer offered sufficient outlet to his precocious physical energy, reacting against the severe admonitions of the straight-laced officers, he gave rein to his natural desires in all manner of vice and ungodliness.'

> It was, she argued, a time which John reflected in his later book *Grace Abounding,* and she quoted the passage: 'Wherefore with more greediness, according to the strength of nature, I did still let loose the reins of my lust and delighted in all transgression against the Law of God... I was the very ringleader of all the Youth that kept me company.'

Some of his men were forced to sleep three in a bed, he wrote to his superiors, adding bitterly: *'There were two in my company that had but one payre of britches betweene them soe that when one was up the other must upon necessity be in his bed.'*

At any rate, as the autumn and winter of 1645 turned into a new year, all of Luke's worst fears about the town's descent into a remaking of Sodom and Gomorrah were returning, and the malaise was not only engulfing Newport.

At Aylesbury, where restless troops had threatened to riot, a period of Martial Law was declared in early 1646 with curfews, fines and jailings and greater powers to back up the regime of Governor Henry Marten.

And now the same regime was imposed at Newport with troop numbers being reduced to 800 and Luke's successor, the over-amiable Col Charles d'Oyley, being replaced by the hard-line zealot Col John Venn.

It was also recorded[30] that Rev Sam Austin, the garrison's long-serving rector was forced out in 1646, perhaps as a result of the escalating decadence but more probably because he became one of an estimated 2,000 Anglican clergymen whose living was sequestrated by Parliament's Committee for Plundered Ministers which replaced them with Puritan or staunchly Protestant believers. Between 20 and 40 were ousted in this way in Buckinghamshire.[31]

---

30 Vera Brittain ibid p88 and elsewhere

31 Prof Ian Beckett, *Guide to Bucks County Museum's Civil War exhibition guide 2001/5*

Seven holy men served the troops

Under Sir Samuel Luke's military Governorship the troops at Newport never lacked for spiritual guidance or religious advice.

The main faiths were Puritan, Protestant and Presbyterian, with some Baptists and Anabaptists. Pacifist Quakers were also said to be tolerated. They were serviced by no fewer than seven 'divines' or holy men who provided two sermons on Sundays and one every Thursday, with prayers and bible readings every morning. And it didn't stop there: before any sizeable skirmish or confrontation a religious service for the troops would be held on the battlefield in advance of a shot being fired, and always a service of thanksgiving would follow for the winning side. Senior officers were themselves expected to preach to their men and to lead them in prayer and the soldiers themselves were generally encouraged to take to the pulpit.

Beside Rev Austin, the seven divines (holy men) at Newport included Rev Thomas Ford, a Presbyterian divine and cousin of Luke, Col Pickering, a popular independent preacher from North Crawley, Edward Harrison, the garrison's treasurer, and Capt Paul Hobson, a senior serving officer.

Austin was replaced as vicar at the parish church of St Peter and St Paul by Rev John Gibbs, an intelligent young Puritan lately graduated from Sidney Sussex College, Cambridge. A number of historians[32] have him being 'newly settled' in the position by the next year (1647) although official records do not have him taking up the parish priesthood until 1648, a position he held for 12 years until he himself was also ousted.

32 F.W.Bull, Carpenter and Vera Brittain.

Inside the Newport garrison, while it was true that the various changes of personnel and the harsher regime cured the worst of the excesses in the short-term, the lack of money for wages was still at the heart of the problem.

Previously, the men at Newport, just like their colleagues at the other Front Line fortresses, had been able to make up some of the shortfall by seizing money, valuables or food and clothing during regular raids on the farms and properties of their enemy. Most officers agreed to 'look the other way' when this seizing or plundering of the *spoils of war*, as it was known, was taking place. But the plain fact was, after three long years of attrition, there was nothing left to take.

▼ **John Bunnion *(sic)* on the muster roll at Newport in 1647.**

Courtesy of the Centre for Bucks Studies.

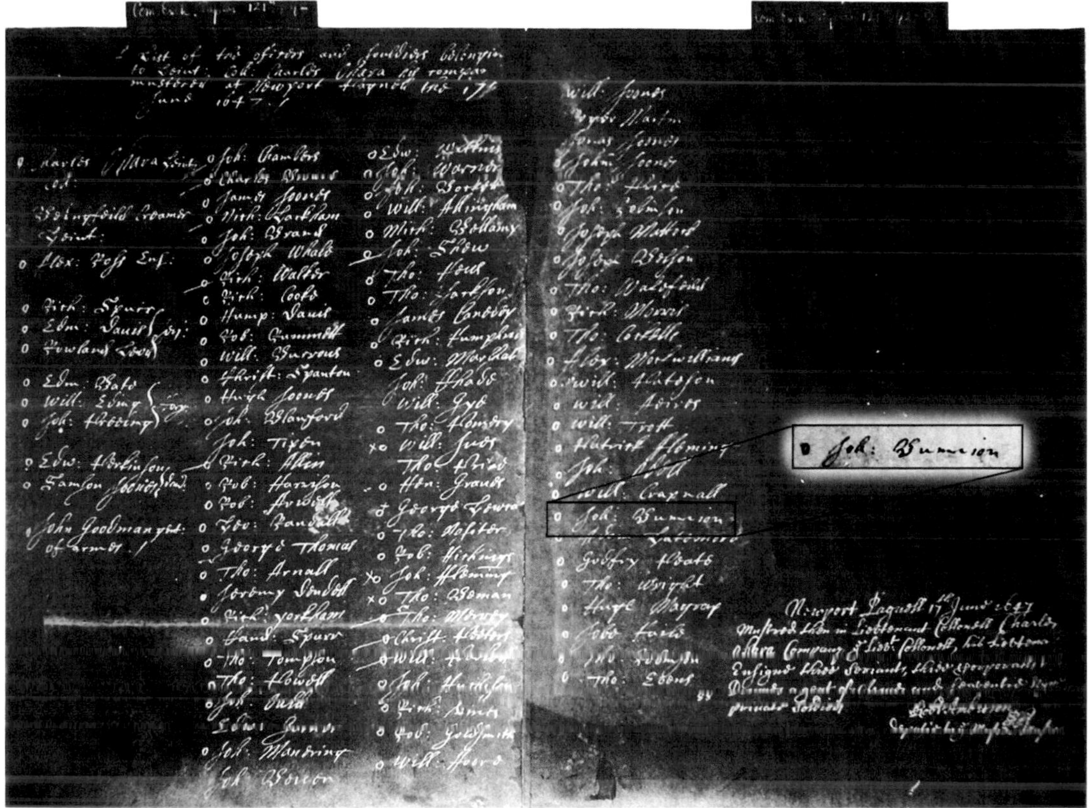

One incident of wanton violence perpetrated by under-employed soldiers on the Vicar of Tyringham, shocked the area early in 1646.[33]

Apparently, the eponymous rector of Tyringham, an elderly neighbour of Lady Digby at Gayhurst, was attacked as he travelled alone near Stony Stratford by Roundhead dragoons who, because they had nothing better to do 'took entertainment' in robbing him of his horse, coat and money and left him with a half-severed arm.

In great pain and despite losing much blood, Rev Anthony Tyringham survived thanks to the skill of surgeons at Aylesbury, although he died a dozen or so years later aged 71 just before achieving his greatest wish of outliving Oliver Cromwell and witnessing the Restoration.

When word of the mindless attack went round it dismayed officers at the Newport garrison but thankfully they did not have long to wait until orders from Parliament's high command in August 1646, decreed that troops there were to be stood down and the fortress walls sleighted. 🔵

Similar instructions went to Bedford, Cambridge and Huntingdon.

In Newport's case the orders specified that guns and powder should be readied for transportation to Ireland where Cromwell planned to mount a campaign, after documents discovered at Naseby revealed that Irish leaders had been secretly trying to reach a pact with the King.

There was also a call for volunteers to join Cromwell's lavish invasion Taskforce with the promise of full wages and any outstanding back-pay settled. The cynical alternative, for those who didn't volunteer, was that their arrears would be lost. Trooper Bunyan, still not aged 19 and thinking there

---

🔵 This order was not carried out until 1648, two years later and the big artillery guns were not removed until 1649

33 *The assault on Rev Tyringham...an incident in North Bucks in 1646 typical of the insecurity of life and property at this time* – a pamphlet transcribed from Archdeacon Bickersteth (archives Bucks County Council)

Is this John Bunyan's mythical view of Newport Pagnell?

The drawing below by Bunyan's friend Robert White (1645–1704) illustrated the celebrated writer's book *The Holy War* (1682). It features a town called Mansoul which scholars suggest was based on Newport Pagnell where Bunyan served as a soldier during more than two-and-a-half years of the Civil War.

FULL-LENGTH PORTRAIT OF JOHN BUNYAN,
By Robert White.
Frontispiece to the First Edition of *The Holy War*, 1682.
[*From the Cambridge Edition of "The Holy War,"* 1905.]

Is it Newport Pagnell? In his review of Bunyan's masterpiece *The Holy War,* Rev John Brown, the 19th century theological historian, was in no doubt. "*Mansoul* – with its walls, gates, stronghold and sallyport (drawbridge) – took shape in his mind from the garrison at Newport Pagnell," he said. He also thought Bunyan's "*Army of Sheddai* – with its forces marching, counter-marching ... dividing, and sub-dividing, closing, wheeling and making good their front and rear – was reminiscent of military manoeuvres in which the young trooper had taken part under Sir Samuel Luke."

Source: *John Bunyan – his Life, Times & Work,* Rev John Brown
(Ballantyne, Hanson 1885; rev 1902)

Sketch file: John Bunyan (1628–1688)

The son of a whitesmith or tinker (repairer of pots and pans) in Bedford who had worked with his father since the age of 10.

His family and that of Rev. John Gibbs, who would later become the parish priest at Newport Pagnell, lived in the same neighbourhood and it is possible that they went to the same school.

In October 1644, then aged almost 16, he either volunteered or was conscripted (ie. 'pressed') to join the Parliamentary forces at the garrison in Newport Pagnell which was considerably under-strength at that time.

According to Muster rolls[34] he was recorded on Nov 30, 1644 under Col Cockayne, March 22, 1645 under Major Boulton and June 17, 1647 under Lt Col Charles O'Hara.

Vera Brittain describes him[35] as a copper-haired youth, tall for

▲   **John Bunyan** – © Bedford Borough Council, Moot Hall, Elstow

his age, vigorous, blue-eyed and long-striding when he marched over from Bedford along the Newport road with a group of other new recruits.

Strong and fit, he soon found that he had joined up during a lull in the action, quickly became bored and turned to taverns in the town to keep himself amused as a ring-leader in fighting, drinking and gambling.

Later, after the euphoria of Naseby had worn off he volunteered to join an advance force heading for Ireland where action was guaranteed but when Cromwell ordered other troops to go there first he was finally stood down in July 1647.

Back in Bedford and back at his old job he soon heard the

first 'inner voices' of a spiritual awakening which would lead him to becoming a prolific writer of Christian stories[36] and catapult him into being one of the most-read authors of all time.

He began preaching on his own account in 1657–8 after writing his first essay/disputation *Some Gospel Truths Opened* and his initial book *A Few Sighs From Hell* published in 1658.

A subsequent title *The Holy War* was the first to reflect his time at the garrison of Newport Pagnell and later books *Grace Abounding* and *Pilgrim's Progress*, his well-known allegorical tales of good triumphing over evil, made him famous.

From 1660, with the Restoration of the Monarchy and concurrent legislation outlawing certain conventicles and preaching, Bunyan would spend the next 12 years in jail at Bedford with frequent visits from Gibbs his lifelong friend when supposedly they drew up plans to 'spread the word' of Calvin's evangelical Protestantism after his release.

---

34 *Baptist Quarterly* magazine Oct 1927, p367 and *John Bunyan, his lifetime & work* Rev John Brown (Ballantyne Hanson & Co, revised 1902)

35 *In the steps of John Bunyan, an excursion into Puritan England* Vera Brittain (Rich & Cowan 1950)

36 *John Bunyan, author* Richard Greaves, ODNB (OUP 2004–12); and others

was not much to return to at Bedford, stepped forward to volunteer and by October found himself with many others on the long march up to Chester where the troops would rendezvous before the crossing from North Wales.

As it turned out, after camping at Chester for six months there came further orders from Command telling the Newport volunteers they would not be needed after all, and they were sent home.

Disappointed by the lack of further action but grateful for the extra pay, Bunyan returned with the party and spent a further three months in the town before being finally laid-off in July 1647, but not before re-establishing his friendship with the town's new young minister, John Gibbs.

On the face of it, the two Johns, Bunyan and Gibbs, seemed an unlikely pair.

On the one hand John Bunyan, the tinker's son and enlisted soldier who had spent his last two-and-a-half years serving in the junior ranks of the force at Newport when most of the fighting was over and had now turned his energies into enjoying the rough and tumble of the town's brothels and drinking dens.

On the other, John Gibbs, almost the same age as Bunyan, who had been to Cambridge by winning one of the few assisted places for the bright children of poorer families, and was now an independent thinker, non-conformist preacher and disciple of the Puritan faith.

Before their lives took them in such different directions it is thought they had been family neighbours in Bedford, and now here they were again, each highly influential on the other and sharing experiences at Newport, that would later provide the material for John Bunyan's allegorical stories of Christian example which would go into millions of homes around the world for many years to come.

The pair would now also cross the path of another friend with the skills to make it all possible, Matthias Cowley, whose family had a business as booksellers and printers in the town, and who was destined to become the first publisher of John Bunyan's works.

More extended essays or disputations than books, these early titles were: *Some gospel truths opened according to the scriptures* ('published by Matthias Cowley in London and Newport Pagnell') in 1656 and *A vindication of some gospel truths opened* ('printed for Matthias Cowley, bookseller in Newport Pagnell') in 1657. Bunyan's third work, *A few sighs from Hell,* contained a prefix message 'to the reader' which was signed JG and is presumed to have been written by John Gibbs.

Painting reveals town link with Reformers

The secret of a 400-year-old painting found at Newport Pagnell's United Reformed Church has revealed another reason why the fortress town was held in such high regard by Oliver Cromwell [37]

The painting was one of five virtually identical

---

37 Sources (courtesy of the URC): An Old Painting – personal notes on the Reformers' Group by Fdk Wm Bull, church notes after the Oxford expert's visit to verify the painting in 1984, and information from Christie's auction catalogue of Feb 23 2005.
Additional: *Samuel Ward* (1572–1643) by Margo Todd (OUP 2004–12); *Secret Sidney,* a brief historical sketch by Richard Humphreys (Sidney Sussex, 2012); *Memorials of Cambridge* by Charles Henry Cooper (Macmillan, 1866), *A brave, bad man: Oliver Cromwell* – article by Cambridge Uni Library (1999), *William Bull, independent minister 1738–1814* by MJ Mercer (ODNB 2004–12); *John Bunyan, author 1628–1688* by Richard Greaves (ODNB 2004–12).

copies of a group of the most important early religious Reformers.

It included familiar Protestant radicals like Bishop John Wycliffe, Martin Luther and John Calvin but uniquely in the Newport version, it also showed the face of another man who had been added in later 'by an unknown hand'. But why – and who was he?

After considerable study, experts were able to identify this extra face as a 16th century theologian by the name of William Perkins ... and now the pieces of a jigsaw that linked him, Oliver Cromwell, a cadre of his top officers, and the vicar of Newport Pagnell, all began to fall into place.

The link was that all of them were connected with Sidney Sussex College at Cambridge, an institution then best-known for its Puritan teachings, exiled Dutchmen, radical politics, and an inn next door called *The Bear* which doubled up as an HQ for the Parliamentary army's Eastern Association.

Who painted the original is not certain ('an unknown artist of the 17th century Anglo-Dutch school,' said the art historians) but Perkins's features gave it a provenance of great interest to Newport Pagnell and especially its involvement in the Civil War.

It is a complicated story and only after studying Perkins' biography does a probable explanation become clear.

The theologian, who lived 1558–1602, was a hugely popular preacher and great

▲ Sidney Sussex College, Cambridge, where both Cromwell and John Gibbs studied

▼ Plaque records Cromwell's head being buried at Sidney Sussex

▲ **The Reformers painting** 🔍 **sold at Christie's. Perkins face has been added in at the back.**
Courtesy of the URC

disciple of the Puritan doctrine which became such a motivating force for Cromwell and the Parliamentarians.

In turn, one of Perkins's keenest admirers was Samuel Ward (1572–1643) another religious academic who went on to become master of Sidney Sussex between 1610–1643, a period of crucial importance to those like Cromwell who studied under him and would become leaders of the uprising that brought down the King.

Another student was Edward Montagu, the 2nd Earl of Manchester, who would become one of the most powerful generals in the Parliamentarian Army. Another was Gen Sir John Reynolds, one of Cromwell's fellow commanders (also see Chapter 7).

And then, hardly a generation later, came young John Gibbs who, after graduating at Sidney Sussex in 1645, was 'intruded' (imposed) as parish priest at Newport from 1648–1660, became the founding minister of what is now the town's United Reformed Church from 1660–1699, and remained a lifelong friend of the one-time garrison soldier John Bunyan.

The painting had been left to the URC by William Bull, the Calvinist minister there from 1764 who was a close friend of Olney's 'Amazing Grace' clergyman John Newton and poet William Cowper.

Minister Bull's son Thomas (1773–1859) and grandson Josiah (1806–1885) continued the family's century-long dynasty during which it ran a college for training independent ministers and was highly influential in the upsurge of evangelical Protestantism in the early 19th century.

🔍 The painting was sold in May 2005 for £4,800 (about double the top estimate) with the money helping to pay for church redevelopment costs.

Chapter 7: Bar the shouting

Town talk in Newport Pagnell during the years 1647–49 was that things might, at long last, be starting to return to normal.

After the euphoria of Naseby in 1645 and the moral mayhem of the following year, calmed only by curfews, Martial Law and a far stricter disciplinary regime, the civilian inhabitants felt that after playing host to a military garrison for the best part of five years, they might now have begun to get their lives back.

Fairfax, Cromwell and the other Parliamentary commanders were taking stock. Charles's army was defeated and dejected, Oxford, his last great bastion had fallen, and the arrogant King had begun his walk along a path that would lead to the executioner's axe.

As 1647 approached, at the Newport stronghold and similarly elsewhere, troop numbers were being reduced. Official orders had been received putting the garrison under notice of disbandment and after a sizeable contingent (including John Bunyan) had marched to Chester for a proposed campaign in Ireland, not much more than a token force was left to ensure military order was maintained.

In front workrooms across the town, ladies must have been dusting down their bobbins and parchment patterns in anticipation of a revival of the cottage lace industry for

The hand-made lace industry was indeed restored in the later years of the War and it continued to bring Newport prosperity until the 1830s when machine-made lace was introduced.

which Newport was already famous; and no doubt the farmers too were restocking their pastures along the fertile Ouse Valley with sheep and cattle to be fattened up for market instead of being requisitioned for the field kitchens of the army.

There was a new man in the pulpit at the parish church. Young John Gibbs, still on the register of the same university college at Cambridge where Cromwell had studied, and brimming with similar Puritan views, had been temporarily 'intruded' ◯ into St Peter & St Paul's in place of the staid and conventional Sam Austin. Next year he would take over officially but already he felt his 'flock was calling' and that they needed him.

Like the nation as a whole, after years in which the ruling establishment and its very way of life had been challenged like never before, there were many in Newport who looked to the new regime for a return to peace and stability.

Yet for those who knew the town's reputation for dissent and non-conformity, few would have been surprised when it found itself caught up in the activities of various radical groups as the Civil War entered a political phase between 1647–49, including a notorious episode which involved a 50-mile manhunt that ended in drama and death on the edge of town.

Ranters, Diggers and Levellers

Scholars who have studied the Civil War in great detail point to it being a unique period in British history in many ways. With the overthrow and then the execution of the King and the abolition of the monarchy it was truly an epoch when, in effect, the people ruled the country through the Parliamentary army.

Never before had the right to free speech been so encouraged. In the army, as in religion, ordinary men were urged to question and debate issues with their officers or, on matters of faith, to preach from the pulpit themselves.

◯ Intruded in this Civil War context meant being *imposed* (on a congregation) without invitation

'It was a time when normal restraints were lifted, a time when it was possible to speak openly, to test barriers, to question authority,' commented one social historian. And so, during this hiatus in the fighting, with no end to it yet declared, groups of men still in, or just out of, the New Model Army now took the opportunity to air their grievances on a variety of social, political and military issues.

With what might be termed left-wing or even communist policies today, one faction, calling themselves the *Diggers,* argued for more land to be taken into common ownership by the people. Another group, the *Ranters,* wanted to promote better communal living based on shared love and understanding, while a third, known as the *Levellers,* by far the most controversial and involving a significant number of serving men, wanted to see a fairer deal for the soldiers.

▲ **Plaque at Burford church records the executed Levellers**

Leveller leaders who gathered support at loose-knit, *ad hoc* meetings in inns and through messages spread by word of mouth and pamphlet, knew they were walking a fine line between the democratic 'freedom to speak' ethos and mutiny.

At Newport there was an involvement with all three radical organisations during those interlude years but it was the *Levellers* who brought it notoriety.

Supporters of the *Ranters* movement caused no harm and brought little aggravation to the people of the town, after all, their main objective was to replace war with love!

No one seemed sure where the *Ranters* had come from. 'Bunyan will have come across this sect in the garrison at Newport Pagnell; it is clear from the correspondence of Sir

Samuel Luke that there was a group in the town. Whether they were indigenous or had drifted down the great road to the Midlands, is hard to say,' concluded one research study later.[38]

It was an emotive group (a fore-runner perhaps of the 'flower power' hippies of San Francisco and the UK in the 1960s) that had promoted the case for sexual liberality and more relaxed morals a couple of years earlier when Governor Luke felt driven to declare that his garrison was fast turning into another Sodom and Gomorrah.

Marilyn Lewis, a minister's wife in the town from the present era, writing about the period,[39] and quoting Professor Christopher Hill of Balliol, Oxford, also suggested that 'free love' was being advocated and that Sir Samuel had confirmed it was being practised in his garrison by the *Ranters* 'whose agenda included attacking traditional beliefs and moral values but who had never formed an organised sect.'

Another group, more numerous than the *Ranters* and increasingly well-supported, were the *Diggers,* labelled with that nickname because of their campaigning for more land to be owned by the community and much less by rich individuals.

In Newport, with its large open areas of Burgh (today Bury) Field, Portsfield and Tickford Field, and now that the fear of military action had receded there was every opportunity for planting and crop laying in the rich, riverside meadows, and cultivation by the *Diggers* had begun there again with 'new' vegetables like cabbages, carrots, sprouts, asparagus and cauliflowers introduced by the large influx of Dutch Protestant immigrants.

These *Digger* communities were proving more and more popular. Probably started in 1648 in Surrey by the visionary Gerrard Winstanley, the concept of communal land holdings

Burgh Field probably derived from Newport being a *burgh* town, ie being one of the Saxons' 'defendable' towns (against the Vikings). It was not, as some supposed, originally named Bury, that name came after almost 700 Great Plague victims were buried there in 'death pits' in 1666. The field is still an open space maintained for the benefit of the townspeople, however Portsfield and Tickford were enclosed in 1795 and 1807 respectively.

---

38 BHRS p46 vol 65, 1986

39 *John Gibbs, a Newport Puritan* by Marilyn Lewis (privately published, 1995)

rapidly gained attraction and there were soon fellow communities at Dunstable[40] in Bedfordshire, Pirton[41] in Hertfordshire, Iver[42] in Buckinghamshire and Wellingborough in Northamptonshire.[43]

Meanwhile, linked to these dissenting groups and, probably the spark which ignited them all, were the *Levellers*.

This faction, which was thought to have its beginnings with a number of disaffected serving soldiers who felt they were being pressed against their will to volunteer for the Irish campaign or lose their outstanding back-pay, was much more of a concern to Fairfax, Cromwell and the Parliamentary army leaders.

A Declaration of the Grounds and Reasons why we the Poor Inhabitants of the Town of *VVellinborrow*, in the County of *Northampton*, have begun and give consent to dig up, manure and sow Corn upon the Common, and waste ground, called *Bareshanke*, belonging to the Inhabitants of *VVellinborrow*, by those that have subscribed, and hundreds more that give Consent.

WE find in the Word of God, that God made the Earth for the use and comfort of all Mankind, and set him in it to till and dresse it, and said, That in the sweat of his brows he should eat his bread; and also we find, that God never gave it to any sort of people, that they should have it all to themselves, and shut out all the rest, but he saith, The Earth hath he given to the children of men, which is every man.

2. We find, that no creature that ever God made was ever deprived of the benefit of the Earth, but Mankind; and that it is nothing but covetousnesse, pride, and hardnesse of heart, that hath caused man so far to degenerate.

3. We find in the Scriptures, that the Prophets and Apostles have left it upon Record, That in the last days the oppressor and proud man shall cease, and God will restore the waste places of the Earth to the use and comfort of Man, and that

▲ **Charter of the Wellingborough *Diggers***

Fuelled by issues about pay, conditions and many broken promises, the movement began in October 1647 when an 'Agreement of the People' was drawn up by a group of rebels led by Thomas Rainborough and John Lilburne after they failed to win concessions in what became known as The Putney Debates. Despite meeting only irregularly these *Levellers* grew in strength until by 1648–9 they had appointed 'agitators' in most NMA regiments and could count on several hundred supporters.

---

40 BHRS vol 65 p48 ibid

41 BHRS ibid p55 note 187

42 *Digger Tracts 1649–50* (London Aporia 1989)

43 *A declaration by the Diggers of Wellinborrow 1649*

They were perceived by senior officers to be 'walking a fine line between acceptable protest and encouraging outright mutiny'.

Perhaps emboldened by the King's demise in January 1649, the *Levellers* attempted to step up their demands with the result, as many had predicted, that Generals Fairfax and Cromwell felt it necessary to bring matters to a head.

After a series of meetings in London in April General Fairfax ordered the execution of *Leveller* Robert Lockyer and sent several others to jail.

In the second week of May came the most serious confrontation when Cromwell and Fairfax, joined now by their colleague Colonel John Reynolds and sections of his cavalry regiment, 'corralled' a group of 340 *Levellers* into the church at Burford, on the north-western side of Oxford, and demanded their surrender.

A stand-off ensued for more than 24 hours but then, with talks breaking down, the commanders ordered three of the rebels, Cornet James Thompson, Corporal Perkins and Private John Church, to be executed by firing squad in front of their colleagues.

Not long afterwards the rest reluctantly gave in, except one, Cornet Thompson's brother James, who made his escape on horseback and set off along Akerman Street with Colonel Reynolds and a detachment of his men in hot pursuit.

Why he chose to flee in that direction is not entirely clear, but it appears from records that Thompson may have decided to head for the *Digger* community at Wellingborough on the far side of Newport Pagnell, where he believed he would find help. Perhaps too, he thought that by crossing into Northamptonshire he might also be safe.

The fugitive's exact route cannot be certain but is most likely to have followed Akerman Street, the ancient Roman track that had become well-known through the war years, skirting the north of Oxford and then taking the fork towards

Bicester and Buckingham as he rode across country to Newport, and Wellingborough beyond.

Cornet Thompson's race for his life along the road to the old garrison town turned into a dramatic manhunt that is remembered in local folklore to this day.

Colonel John Reynolds led the hunt for William Thompson

An account by the Royal Historical Society[44] describes how, being cornered in woods between Newport and Wellingborough: 'He died fighting with a courage worthy of a better cause.'

At first, says the RHS, Thompson, alone but mounted on his horse, charged straight at Colonel Reynolds and his party, shooting one soldier and wounding another before being hit twice himself and retreating.

Then, as they got near him once more, he charged again with his pistol and received another shot before retreating.

Finally, and after refusing an offer to *take quarter* (surrender), the end came when he charged for a third time. The RHS account concludes matter of factly: 'Major Butler's corporal holding Colonel Reynolds carbine with seven bullets, gave Thompson his death wound.'

- On May 25, 1649 Cromwell reported to Parliament on 'the successful suppression' of the *Levellers*[45]

- In July 1649 Colonel Reynolds left for Ireland to lead an advance invasion force[46]

- At least 200,000 soldiers and civilians are thought to have died in Cromwell's Irish campaign from war or war-related causes. New Model Army casualties were about 8,000.

---

44 *Transactions of the Royal Historical Society* vol XV (RHS, London 1901) with *History of Banbury* (Beesly, p438–445)

45 *The Leveller Mutinies* by David Plant (web, 2005)

46 Biography of Sir John Reynolds by David Plant

Postscript

Although beyond the scope of this book there was an amusing incident at Newport just before the end of the Commonwealth period that will be of interest.

After Oliver Cromwell's death in 1658 and the short, unsatisfactory rule of his son Richard that ended in his abdication in the following year, there were a number of Royalist uprisings across the country.

None were successful and one, led by Sir George Booth, had a farcical ending worthy of the West End stage.

Defeated in Chester by Col. John Lambert, Booth fled the scene dressed as a woman and tried to make it down to London with four companions, but they reckoned without the sharp eyes of the landlord of the Red Lion (as then was) at the bottom of High Street.

According to the records of Sir William Clarke,[47] a civil servant at the time, one of the maids at the inn noticed that guest 'Mrs Dorothy' had abnormally large feet and 'Dorothy's' cover was blown completely when another maid peeked through a crack in the door and spotted him shaving.

At this, regaled Sir William, *'the master of the inne sent for 10 neighbours (including the vicar John Gibbs, it transpired) who, armeing themselves, breake open Mrs Dorothy's chamber door about one in the morneing and demaunded what she was.'*

Sir William's account continues that the good people of Newport, hospitable as ever, bought the fugitive some men's clothes, a hat and some new boots before packing him off under armed guard to London and the Tower.

But the story didn't end there.

According to a subsequent edition of the *Baptist Quarterly* magazine[48] Rev Gibbs then got on his horse and rode off

▲ **Sir George Booth, alias Mrs Dorothy**

From a painting by Dunham Massey

---

47 *The Clarke papers* vol 4 para 239 ed. C H Firth (Camden Soc., 1901)

48 *Baptist Quarterly* pp315–322 John Gibbs by Maurice F Hewett

to the House of Commons 'to communicate the earliest intelligence of this event' and, having told the MPs what happened, was pleased when, 'a pecuniary reward' was voted to him and the others concerned.

Mind you, Sir George was not in prison for long.

In 1660, just a few months later and with the Royals returning, another source[49] reported that he was 'zealously employed in bringing about the Restoration of the Stuarts to the throne of England.'

Now it was his turn to be rewarded as the new pro-monarchy Parliament voted him £10,000 from the public purse and the new King, Charles II elevated him to the peerage as Lord Delamer.

◄ Tablet remembers Gibbs' 12 years as Vicar of Newport and 38 years as minister of today's United Reformed Church

---

49 *Newport Pagnell and its neighbourhood*, Joseph Simpson (Simpson & Sons, NPagnell, 1887)

Sketch file: Rev John Gibbs (1627–1699)

John Gibbs was leader of the religious community in Newport during the garrison's most morally testing time in the Civil War and was an influential figure in the town for more than 50 years.

The son of a cooper and local councillor in Bedford it is 'generally supposed'[50] that Gibbs, then a young Puritan convert, became vicar of Newport in 1646 as the Parliamentary committee's choice to replace the conventional Rev Samuel Austin.

Aged just 19, Gibbs was only partway through his studies at the Cambridge University college attended by Oliver Cromwell and several other of his senior officers. He does not seem to have taken up the position at Newport officially until 1648 but in the meanwhile he found himself caught up in the period of moral and social upheaval at the garrison when the soldiers 'grew bored and restless' after the euphoria of their success at Naseby.

The relationship between Gibbs and John Bunyan, a conscripted trooper at the fortress, grew close during this time and they remained lifelong friends.

Described as having well-cultivated intelligence, a wonderful memory, acute judgement, eminent piety and great integrity,[51] he could also be vexatious, 'lean and lone' and argumentative.

Rev Gibbs was himself ejected from the parish church in 1660 at the Restoration, but tradition has it that he simply walked a short way down the High Street and founded an 'independent chapel' in a supporter's barn (today's United Reformed Church).

For the next nearly 40 years he became an influential figure in dissenting church circles, suffering persecution, ill-treatment and spells of imprisonment when the authorities banned certain assemblies and preaching as unlawful.

His was a truly independent spirit as evidenced by documents and licences which described him at different times as a Protestant minister, Congregationalist, Presbyterian, Baptist and Anabaptist, and with a village circuit as a barn preacher that included Olney, Newton Blossomville, Cranfield, Astwood and Roade.

Gibbs stayed close to John Bunyan as a friend and adviser throughout the writer's regular periods in Bedford jail and it is said that during his visits the pair used their time to plan how to spread the word of Calvin's evangelical Protestantism beginning with Bedford, Wellingborough, Northampton, Cambridge, and of course, Newport Pagnell.[52]

Rev Gibbs was survived by his wife Martha and their

▲ Gibbs's gravestone as it is today with just a plain, brief inscription in the parish churchyard

---

50 Transactions of the Congregational Hist Soc. vol 10 1927, & elsewhere

51 From Rev Gibbs' original tombstone outside the south door of the parish church and translated from the Latin

52 See Bunyan Sketch file on page 90

Selected bibliography

Recommended reading includes the following, in addition to works mentioned in text:

In the steps of John Bunyan, an excursion into Puritan England, Vera Brittain (Rich & Cowan 1950)

Buckinghamshire Biographies – a schoolbook, Margaret Verney (Clarendon Press, 1912)

John Gibbs, a Newport Pagnell Puritan, Mary Lewis (privately published, 1995)

A History of Newport Pagnell, Frederick William Bull (W E & J Goss, 1900)

The Garrison of Newport Pagnell during the Civil Wars, Rev H Roundell (BAS Records of Bucks 1859-1862 vol 2)

John Bunyan – his Life, Times & Work, Rev John Brown (Ballantyne, Hanson 1885 & 1902)

The Letterbooks of Sir Samuel Luke 1644–5, ed. H G Tibbutt (HMSO, 1963)

Sir Samuel Luke 1603–1670 (ODNB 2004–10)

Sir John Digby 1605–1645 (ODNB 2004–11)

John Thurloe 1616–1668 (ODNB 2007)

George Booth 1622–1684 (ODNB 2004–11)

Sir Lewis Dyve 1599–1669 (ODNB 2004–9)

Major Gen Philip Skippon ?–1660 (ODNB 2004–9)

Dr Henry Atkins 1554/5–1635 (ODNB 2004–11)

John Venn, regicide 1586–1650 (ODNB 1899)

Samuel Butler abt 1613–1680 (ODNB 2004–10)

George Digby 1612–1677 (ODNB 2004–9)

Sir Everard Digby c.1578–1606 (ODNB 2004–9)

Sir Kenelm Digby 1603–1665 (ODNB 2004–9)

Prince Rupert 1619–1682, Ian Roy (ODNB 2004–9)

Thomas Fairfax 1612–1671, Ian Gentles (ODNB 2004–9)

William Bull 1738–1814, M J Mercer (ODNB 2004–12)

John Bunyan 1628–1688, Richard Greaves (ODNB 2004–12)

Gervase Pagnell, Mary Bateson (ODNB 1885–1900 vol 43)

The Life of John Thurloe, VCH compid 55221 and VCH: Bucks vol 4 (1927) pp409–422

The Clarke Papers (Camden Society, 1901)

The town of Newport Pagnell and its neighbourhood, Joseph Simpson (Simpson & Sons, Newport Pagnell, 1868)

Bedfordshire before the Civil War (BHRS vol 65, 1986)

Sales of Royalist Land during the interregnum, Joan Thirsk (Economic History Review, new series 1952)

Law and Local society in the time of Charles I, Ross Lee (BHRS)

The Life & Letters of Sir Lewis Dyve, H G Tibbutt (the Society of Streatley, Beds, 1948)

Cromwell, our chief of men, Antonia Fraser (Panther, 1975)

Memoirs of Sir Samuel Luke (Gentleman's magazine 1823 vol 93 Pt II pp28–31 and 1835 pp28 et seq)

History & topography of Buckinghamshire, James Sheahan (pub. unknown, 1862)

Sherington Historical Society (newsletters, various)

The Gunpowder Plot Society (articles, various)

Going to the Wars, Charles Carlton (Routledge, 1992)

Akeman Street, Tim Copeland (History Press, Stroud 2009)

A History of the Life of Col. Nathaniel Whetham, Catherine Dampier (Longmans, Green & Co 1907)

A History of Antiquities of the County of Buckingham, vol iv, ed. George Lipscomb (Bowyer Nicholas, London 1831)

Life of Sir John Digby, ed. George Bernard (Royal Historical Soc., Paris, 1910)

Haunted Places in Newport Pagnell, Julie Wilson (Victoria pub, 2011)

Grafton Regis: the history of a Northamptonshire village, eds Charles FitzRoy & Keith Harry (Merton Priory Press, 2000)

One More for the Road, Donald Hurst & Dennis Mynard (Southgate pub 1999)

Driven Together, Richard Meredith (Mercury Books for Word Go 2008)

Olney Bridge (Bucks Standard, Jan 4 1974)

Grafton Estate catalogue papers (esp refs 401–600 at Northampton Records Office)

House of Cromwell: a genealogical history of the family and descendants, James Waylen (E Stock, 1897)

The Parliament Scout, March 15–22, 1644

Masters of Foxhounds Association directory, refs Grafton, Heythrop and Whaddon Chase hunts

A short history of Bernwood Forest (Bucks CC, 2005)

History of the County of Buckingham, vol 4 1927, N Crawley pp327–8, Hillesden pp173–180

Influence of Low Dutch on the English, E C Llewellyn (OUP, 1936)

History of the County of Northampton, vol 5 2002 ref Grafton Regis pp142–176

Some account of the town of Buckingham, Rev Henry Roundell (Cavalot, reprinted 1989)

Battles & Generals of the Civil Wars 1642–51, HCB Rogers

Grafton Regis History & Heritage (Millenium Committee, 2004)

The history of Newport Pagnell, Staines (1842)

Sherington – fiefs & fields of a Buckinghamshire village, A C Chibnall (CUP, 1965)

Newport Pagnell – historic town assessment report

(drafts from Sept 2010) – compilers Bucks CC and MKC

Stony Stratford: The last skirmish, Paul Woodfield
(Festival 350, 1994)

Story of the Congregational Church Newport Pagnell,
Rev R G Martin (1960)

History & Antiquities of the Newport Pagnell Hundreds,
Oliver Ratcliff (Cowper Press, 1900)

Early Reformers: all Wikipedia: John Harley, bishop d.1558;
Lawrence Humphrey abt 1527–1590; Lollardy and John
Wycliffe; Phillip Melanchthon 1497–1560; Huldrych Zwingli
1484–1531; William Perkins 1558–1602

Quakerism at Hogstye End, Tyeth Spencer
(Leighton Buzzard Obs. 1938)

*The Organizational Response of non-conformity to repression
& indulgence: The case for Bedfordshire,* Richard A Greaves
(Cambridge Journals pp472–484)

Samuel Ward (1572–1643) by Margo Todd (OUP 2004–12)

Secret Sidney, a brief historical sketch, Richard Humphreys
(Sidney Sussex, 2012)

Memorials of Cambridge, Charles Henry Cooper
(Macmillan, 1866)

A brave, bad man: Oliver Cromwell, article by Cambridge
University Library (1999).

Rupert, Prince Palatine, Eva Scott (Archibald Constable
& Co 1900)

Romance of the Lace Pillow, Thomas Wright (Paul Minet, 1971)